# POLITICS
# AND THE
# BIBLICAL
# DRAMA

# POLITICS AND THE BIBLICAL DRAMA

by

## RICHARD J. MOUW

WILLIAM B. EERDMANS PUBLISHING COMPANY

Printed in the United States of America


**Library of Congress Cataloging in Publication Data**

Mouw, Richard J.
    Politics and the Biblical drama.

    1. Christianity and politics.    2. Bible—Political
science.    I. Title.
BR115.P7M593        261.7        76-25004
ISBN 0-8028-1657-6

# CONTENTS

Preface                                              7

1. THE TASK OF POLITICAL THEOLOGY                    9
   The Bible and Political Reflection               11
   The Scope of Political Theology                  13
   Some Current Questions                           15
   The Biblical Drama                               18

2. CREATION AND HUMAN SOCIETY                        21
   The Image of God                                 22
   Created Sociality                                29
   Created Politics?                                32

3. SIN AND POLITICS                                  37
   Two Serpentine Falsehoods                        39
   Sin and Selfishness                              41
   Sin and Manipulation                             45
   Sinful Politics                                  48
   The Divine Response                              52

4. REDEEMED SOCIETY: THE CHURCH'S
   LIFE AND MISSION                                 55

The "Marks of the True Church"                        57
The Scope of Christian Community                      59
Church and Kingdom                                    63
The "External" Mission                                67
Identifying with Oppression                           70
Serving the Poor                                      74
The Concern for Justice                               77
A Complex Mission                                     80

**5. CONFRONTING THE "POWERS"**                       85

"Principalities and Powers"                           85
Disputes about the Powers                             90
Some Additional Problems                              92
The Powers and Political Involvement                  97
The Anabaptist-Reformed Dialogue                      98
"Revolutionary Subordination"                        100
The Refusal to "Manage Society"                      107
"Accepting Powerlessness"                            111

**6. POLITICS AND THE COMING KINGDOM**               117

Dispensationalist "Israel-Monism"                    118
Finding Babylon Today                                124
The Future of "the Kings of the Earth"               129
"The Glory and the Honor of the Nations"             135
The Transformation of Politics                       137

*Indexes*                                            140

# PREFACE

During the past three years I helped to draft and placed my signature on two public statements: the 1973 Chicago Declaration of Evangelical Social Concern, and the 1975 Hartford Appeal for Theological Affirmation. The first document was greeted in many religious quarters as signaling a major commitment to political activism on the part of "conservative evangelical" Christians. The second statement was widely interpreted — often by the same persons who had shown enthusiasm for the Chicago document — as a call for "retreat" from Christian political involvement.

My continuing and firm endorsement of both public statements is based on the conviction that together they form a coherent and balanced position with respect to Christian political thought and action. To submit to the lordship of Jesus Christ is to become committed to the political dimensions of his lordship. But this commitment must also be carried out with critical reflection, lest our professions of political obedience become disguises for one or another of the subtle forms of "cultural captivity" which regularly threaten the Christian community. Christian political activism cannot be divorced from an engagement in careful theological reflection. Orthodoxy without ortho-praxy may be dead, as we have been constantly reminded in recent years; but the latter without the former will quickly slip into mindlessness, a quality which at least matches dead orthodoxy as a corrupting influence among Christians. I hope this book will serve as a contribution to the important Christian enterprise of *mindful activism.*

Much of the material in the following pages was first presented in a series of lectures to the students and faculty of Regent College in Vancouver during January 1975; I am indebted to them for their helpful responses to those lectures, and to the Staley Foundation for sponsoring that visit. I am also indebted to my colleagues in the Calvin College philosophy department for their careful criticisms of earlier versions of chapters two and five, to Neal Plantinga who read the penultimate draft of the entire manuscript; and to my colleagues at *The Reformed Journal,* especially Nicholas Wolterstorff and Marlin Van Elderen, who contribute much to my own political and theological interests. While I am primarily responsible for choosing the topics and formulating the arguments which appear in these pages, my philosophical and journalistic colleagues in Grand Rapids must also be held responsible for any basic defects in the general *drift* of my discussion.

The final version of this manuscript was produced in very cramped living conditions in a small apartment in Princeton, New Jersey. Phyllis and Dirk will understand why this circumstance necessitates my expressions of grati-tude and apology to them.

Finally, these words are being written during a period that coincides with the retirement of William Spoelhof as President of Calvin College. He has demonstrated to me, and to many others, the possibilities for integrating aca-demic "politics" with Christian conviction and kindness — thus he has been an important example of the way in which the Word can take on administrative flesh. For this, and for many other things, I offer him my heartfelt thanks.

R. J. M.

# CHAPTER ONE

# THE TASK OF POLITICAL THEOLOGY

This book is an exercise in "political theology." The themes and emphases that have come to be associated with this label in recent years have been greeted with varying degrees of enthusiasm in the Christian community; indeed, there are some who insist that the label itself is based on a confused understanding of the proper scope of theology. In spite of these misgivings the label is an appropriate means of designating the discussion that will be pursued in these pages.

It is easy to sympathize with some of the criticisms which have been lodged against much recent political theology. Carl Henry is correct in complaining that the writings that fall under this rubric are often very "man-centered" and are frequently too closely aligned with Marxist theories. But Henry is less convincing when he suggests that "it is unclear how much of this political emphasis is properly designated theology, in view of the primary concern of theology with the knowledge of God."[1]

This objection goes much further than a mere com-

---

[1]"Political Theology," in C. F. H. Henry (ed.), *Baker's Dictionary of Christian Ethics* (Grand Rapids: Baker, 1973), p. 514.

plaint about the actual products of the enterprise of political theology; it suggests that the very conjunction of the terms "political" and "theology" is a mismatch. To counter Henry's objection we need not dispute his insistence that theology has to do with "the knowledge of God"; for even when we acknowledge this to be the central concern of the theological enterprise, there are important respects in which political concerns cannot be divorced from theology.

First, since the task of theology has to do with the knowledge of the God who reveals his will in and through the Scriptures, we cannot ignore, in our theology proper, the manner in which political concerns pervade the biblical narrative. The Bible does not disregard the participation of the human beings to whom God reveals himself in political affairs. God's promise to bless the descendants of Abraham included references to their political well-being; when the Israelites were rescued out of Egypt, the bonds of their political oppression had to be broken; the psalmists wrote political prayers; the prophets delivered messages about political policies; Jesus faced political temptations; apocalyptic visions include political scenarios. Thus Christians who profess a high view of the integrity of the biblical message could be expected to have a particular interest in political matters.

Second, the Bible does more than merely picture human beings as involved in political relationships; it applies political categories to God himself. It does so directly, by referring to him as "ruler" and "king"; but it also does so by implication. If God is all powerful, for example, it is necessary to ask how the power of earthly rulers is to be assessed with reference to his power; if God is just, we are compelled to inquire whether human patterns of political justice compare favorably with divine standards.

The fact is that the "knowledge of God" toward which theology aims is very broad in its dimensions. It is a knowledge of the God who has revealed the riches of his grace in response to the full scope of our sinful predicament. Any account of human sin which leaves out a reference to the manifestations of human rebellion in the political realm is thereby an impoverished one. And from this it follows that any view of God that fails to acknowledge him as a political redeemer is also inadequate.

Third, Henry's objection, taken seriously, would put more restrictions on the theological task than would seem to be desirable. If Christology is a proper division of theology, how can we avoid the political dimensions of the early church's confession that Jesus is Lord and King? Similarly, the concept of "the Kingdom of God" is central to discussions in eschatology. Even if one suspects that the political connotations of many traditional theological concepts are only apparent ones — so that we would have to divest such terms as "ruler," "kingdom," and "lord" of their ordinary meanings when engaging in theological discussion — this is something that would require careful demonstration, not simply an assumption with which to begin. Even if a completely "apolitical" theology is possible, then, we could only attain it by engaging in a lengthy discussion of political concepts — for no other reason than finally to purge them from our theology.

There is no reason, however, to assume that it is proper to desire an "apolitical" theology. Rather, we would do well to take seriously the fact that political references of various sorts are woven into the biblical narrative. But how ought we to go about the business of taking the political message of the Scriptures seriously?

## THE BIBLE AND POLITICAL REFLECTION

The Bible is the locus and record of God's address to human beings in their "wholeness," including the entire network of relationships, institutions, and projects in which they participate. The biblical message, then, addresses our political lives.

But the Bible is not a systematic treatise on political theory. Indeed, it is not a systematic treatise on *any* subject. The biblical message is an urgent word from God, a word that speaks of sin and grace, judgment and redemption. This word does not provide us with a theory about marriage, but it does address women and men in their roles as wives and husbands. It offers no philosophy of labor and management, but it invites human beings to pursue their vocations in obedience to the will of God. It is not a technical account of the role of government, but it calls citizens and rulers to repentance.

But if we cannot derive answers to fundamental questions about society and politics by strict deduction or inference from the Bible, neither can we set the Scriptures aside as irrelevant to our reflections on these matters. Instead, we must attempt to address these topics as persons who are aware of the fact that the Bible has spoken to us in the "wholeness" of our lives, including our political lives. We must attempt to speak about political matters out of minds and hearts disciplined by the word from God. Our political thoughts must be developed to the point where they are fitting ones for people who confess obedience to the will of God.

One way of putting the point here is that the Christian community, and particularly the theological practitioners within it, must engage in a very complex conversation in the presence of the word. As an indispensable element in this conversation, the Christian community must observe and listen to what is going on in the political realm, in order to become sensitive to the variety of questions and answers — both theoretical and practical — being articulated there. Because of the crucial need for this kind of listening posture, we can sympathize with Gustavo Gutierrez's call for a political theology which is a "critical reflection on historical praxis."[2] Political theology must be directed toward political service on the part of the church, which is in turn a response to the actual political needs of the world.

But political theology must also include, as Gutierrez

[2] *A Theology of Liberation*, tr. and ed. by Sister Caridad Inda and John Eagleson (Maryknoll, N. Y.: Orbis, 1973), p. 15.

rightly puts it, "critical reflection" on those political needs. The church cannot simply provide whatever the world is asking for; it must respond to the world in a manner faithful to the word it has received. When we sing in the familiar carol that "the hopes and fears of all the years" were met in Bethlehem on the first Christmas, we are not offering a *carte blanche* fulfilment of all the hopes and fears that are actually felt in the world. The redemptive work of Christ does not *simply* dissolve the hopes and fears of a Cain or a Herod or a Richard Burton. The biblical message is "good news" only if we are willing to receive it by responding with repentance to the theme of judgment it includes. The hopes and fears of the world are properly met only when they are correctly interpreted and judged in the light of the gospel.

## THE SCOPE OF POLITICAL THEOLOGY

Properly understood, the task of the political theologian is as broad as the scope of theology itself. In order to see why this is so, we must briefly note some essential elements in the overall enterprise of theology.

If Christian theology is to be faithful to God's revelation of his will for his creation, it must center on the study of Holy Scripture. At the basis of all Christian theological reflection, then, is *biblical theology,* an activity which includes the critical study of specific texts and the attempt to articulate generalizations formed on the basis of studying those texts. Thus, a biblical theologian might begin a given study by exegeting some passages from Joel and Amos, then go on to claim that in the minor prophets — or even in the Old Testament as a whole — there is a tension between certain themes.

*Systematic theology* is a further reflection on the inductive generalizations of biblical theology. It is pursued for the purpose of finding more precise interrelationships among those generalizations. To the degree that the biblical data themselves permit it, one can hope here for a "systematizing" or a logically coherent "packaging" of what the Bible says.

The results of both biblical and systematic theology can be pursued in at least two further directions. *Practical theology* seeks to provide the foundations for applying biblical concerns to preaching, evangelism, counseling, and the like. *Philosophical theology*, which includes *apologetics*, attempts to articulate and clarify the claims of biblical and systematic theology in the context of "secular" intellectual discussion.

This curricular sketch of the theological enterprise is stated here in an oversimplified form. For one thing, it leaves out reference to the crucial dependence of theology on such supporting disciplines as language study and history. Furthermore, theology as a whole is a much more "dynamic" enterprise than this sketch would indicate: the task of the biblical exegete, for example, requires the use of hermeneutical principles which depend in turn on systematic and philosophical theology for their formulation; confessional perspectives also enter in at every point. This kind of interaction among various levels of theological focus cannot be avoided. Thus, the insistence by some Christians that they are (in contrast to everyone else) "simply taking the Bible at its word" is a delusion. All we can do is honestly to acknowledge the complexities of theological reflection, with the hope that we will be open to necessary corrections and revisions.

It must also be observed that the subject matter of theology can be divided up in other legitimate ways. For our purposes, however, this way of stating the case will provide a helpful means of viewing the task of political theology. As it turns out, a properly formed political theology, developed to its fullest proportions, will have to contain each of the elements necessary to the overall theological task as we have sketched it above. If political theology is to be an adequate expression of the conviction that the Scriptures are the record and locus of God's unique revelation to humanity, including political humanity, the work of biblical theology will be fundamental to the enterprise: a biblically faithful political theology cannot be carried on apart from considering those biblical texts which relate, directly or indirectly, to political matters.

*Biblical political theology*, then, must be the touchstone for any *systematic political theology* that we might develop. And if a systematizing of biblical political data can be achieved, the implications of this body of doctrine must be spelled out in terms of a *practical political theology*, which would provide guidelines for political preaching, counseling, and mission.[3] Finally, political theology should include a dimension that can be labeled *philosophical political theology*, in the pursuit of which we take seriously the challenges and questions posed by secular theoretical perspectives and the ongoing cultural dialogue.

Here, too, we must insist on the dynamic character of the theological enterprise. We must not expect that any segment of the political theological task can be addressed in isolation from the others. Nor, on the other hand, should we expect any specific exercise in political theology to give equal time to all of these dimensions of the task.

Our discussion in this book will touch on each of these areas, although we will not be concerned to identify the specific dimension being touched on at each point. The purpose in distinguishing these various stages of the political theological task is to point to complexities involved in Christian political reflection. This present discussion can only be intended as a modest contribution to a part of that task.

## SOME CURRENT QUESTIONS

We have already indicated that political theology, if it is going to provide an adequate address to the current

[3]I would classify my previous work, *Political Evangelism* (Grand Rapids: Eerdmans, 1973), under the rubric of "practical political theology."

cultural situation, must include a listening dimension. It must address itself to the actual questions being asked.

When we listen to the cultural/political dialogue which characterizes our present situation it is difficult to avoid the impression that Western culture is experiencing a mood of political and institutional disillusionment. During recent decades this mood has often expressed itself in challenges to traditional modes of human interaction and sometimes by accompanying proposals for restructuring those arrangements: What is a family? Is it necessarily or ideally a father, a mother, and one or more children living under one roof? Or are extended communal "families" possible and even desirable? What is a marriage? Does cohabitation on the part of two homosexuals count as such? Can an "open marriage" survive? What is a classroom? Should we view it merely as a means whereby children "internalize" assigned socio-economic roles? Should we seek to make it function effectively as an arena for "self-realization?" What is a church? Would "household churches" be more effective in promoting proper worship? Ought we to have ministers and priests and rabbis in the traditional sense?

Closely related to these discussions and the experiments that have arisen as a result there has been increasing interest in the nature and extent of the "political" dimensions of human relationships. One result of this interest is seen in the recent expansion of the meaning of the term "politics"—whereby various kinds of social interactions have been labeled political in a manner that would have been incomprehensible in the past.

Consider as an example the trend toward merging the language of sex with the language of politics. From one direction, there has been a growing tendency to describe political phenomena in sexual terms. Confirmation can be found in both the White House tapes that led to Richard Nixon's downfall and in the graffiti of the radicals whom he perceived as his enemies, not to mention the "rape of the earth" theme prominent in the ecology movement. From the other direction, there has been an increasing application of political terminology to sexual relations. The titles of books and articles indicate this trend: "Sex and Power," "The Politics of Touch," "The Politics of the Orgasm," "The Ideology of the Family."

What is going on when someone describes the marital bed as a "political arena?" Such an observation is a case in point of a more general concern about patterns of authority and access to decision-making power. In the past, discussion of political relationships tended to be limited to fairly explicit patterns of authority and power in the area of civil government; other uses of political terms (e.g., "office politics") were seen as metaphorical or humorous. Today the language of politics has come to be applied with serious persistence to a wide variety of authority-patterns. There has been a special sensitivity to the way in which these patterns are perpetuated in less than fully conscious ways through words and gestures. Thus, describing fifty-year-old women secretaries as "the girls at the office" is viewed as signaling an inferior role-assignment; the way men and women congregate at cocktail parties and their "body language" is taken to reveal something about acceptable decision-making patterns in the group; talk of "the guys in the white hats" is interpreted as a vehicle for perpetuating sexist and racist stereotypes.

Such analyses can be illuminating and helpful. Important questions may arise, however, when we see what kind of changes in our social arrangements they call for. Some assume the kind of ideal associated with the hope for a "withering away of the state." From this perspective, what is valued is a "depoliticizing" of all human relationships, the ultimate goal being an unregulated, spontaneous harmony. On this view all patterns of power and authority are viewed as manipulative and coercive. For others, the analysis of the dynamics of social interaction can be accepted as illuminating, but what it illuminates is a set of patterns considered to be, for various reasons, unalterable. Still others would insist that it is not an elimination of patterns of authority and decision-making that is necessary, but a humanization of them, restructuring them along more just and equitable lines.

What is at stake here, then, are variations on the fundamental questions of classical political thought: What is the ground or purpose of social relationships as such? How, if at all, can political patterns make a positive contribution to such relationships? What kinds of political patterns will do that best?

Christians have also been asking these questions and engaging in these conceptual explorations. This is due in part to the fact that the Christian community has not escaped the widespread mood of disillusionment. A rethinking of traditional political attitudes has been taking place in almost every segment of the Christian community. The problems being raised in the cultural dialogue are not only to be dealt with for evangelistic purposes; they occasion a call for serious pastoral concern.

## THE BIBLICAL DRAMA

If we are going to pursue the task of political theology, we cannot help being influenced by these widespread concerns. But we must also allow our response to them to be shaped and disciplined by the biblical message.

The Scriptures tell a long and complicated story about God's dealings with his creation, but the major elements can be summarized as follows: In the beginning God created human beings to live in the world that he had made. The situation originally was a very happy one. Certain patterns of authority and accountability were spelled out, and as long as human beings recognized and respected this state of affairs, things proceeded in a harmonious fashion. But human rebellion entered the picture and things changed drastically. Moral and social barriers arose — between God and human beings, and among human beings themselves. The situation seemed hopeless because human beings are incapable of breaking down these barriers. But God is not helpless, and he has initiated a new approach in divine-human relations. Ultimately, God himself became a human being, and he acted decisively to restore the original state of affairs. Because of what God has done, a favorable outcome is now certain; but the process of restoration is a slow and painful one. The situation is further complicated by the fact that many human beings refuse to accept, or even to acknowledge, that God has initiated a new relationship. The favorable outcome, then, cannot be completely secured until this continued rebellion is finally eradicated. When that happens, there will be a new order of perfection and harmony.

This, in very brief form, is a summary of the biblical plot. Most Christians would agree with the way in which we have summarized the story; but they would soon discover disagreements emerging when they began to discuss how social and political patterns fit into the picture at various stages of the drama. Some would say that in a significant sense political patterns and a kind of social order were an important part of the original unfallen creation. Others would insist that what we refer to when we speak of politics came on the scene only after the appearance of human sin, as a remedy for human rebellion. Still others would argue that while politics must be viewed as a sinful phenomenon, there is nothing at all remedial about political structures—they are merely a regrettable feature of a sinful world from which Christians must dissociate themselves. The discussion gets even more complicated when we ask what kind of political involvement, if any, is a legitimate mode of Christian activity.

We will be concerned about these and other issues as we reflect on the biblical drama. The complications and subtleties involved make it necessary to organize our discussion around a distinction among four stages, or conditions, in the biblical drama: creation, fall, redemption and the future age. We must ask what, if anything, politics has to do with each of these stages: Was the Garden of Eden an apolitical situation? Are political structures purely fallen elements in human social life? Is political activity compatible with the redeemed patterns of Christian discipleship? Will the final return of Christ bring about a destruction of the present political order?

These questions signal many points of significant disagreement among Christians. If we cannot solve all difficulties to everyone's satisfaction in the following pages, it is hoped that we can at least shed light on some of the differences in understanding the proper shape of the current life and mission of the redeemed people of God.

# CHAPTER TWO

# CREATION AND HUMAN SOCIETY

Political philosophers have devoted considerable attention to fundamental questions about society and politics. They have asked how social and political arrangements relate to their basic accounts of human nature, and they have investigated the point of positive social arrangements as such and the ground of political obligation.

These are important matters which are very much akin to our present concerns. But from a Christian perspective these questions, as they are normally asked by political theorists, often have a puzzling ring to them. We have already indicated the source for this puzzlement. The Christian cannot ask about social and political arrangements in the light of human nature without introducing some immediate qualifications: human nature as viewed from which of the conditions portrayed in the biblical drama? It is one thing to ask how political arrangements enter into the life of fallen humanity, but does the answer to this question tell us anything about the place of politics in human relationships as originally intended by God?

In this chapter we will discuss the function of society and politics in the unfallen creation as pictured in the first few chapters of Genesis. Unfortunately, what we find there are at best hints at plausible answers to our questions. But we can learn something by at least pursuing these hints, with the legitimate expectation that an examination of the other three stages (fall, redemption, and future age) will cast additional light on the concerns of this chapter. Our subsequent examination of the way in which the fallen condition is portrayed should reveal something about what was lost or perverted because of the entrance of sin into human affairs; the topic of redemption should provide indications as to what gets restored or reclaimed through God's redemptive initiative; and biblical visions of the coming age tell us something about what the creation will be like when sin is no longer present in it. In a sense, then, all four conditions must be taken into account if we are to discern God's creative purposes.

## THE IMAGE OF GOD

What is the basis for forming social arrangements in the light of the creation account? In philosophical tradition there have been at least two different schools of thought as to why human beings participate in positive social relationships. Some philosophers view human beings as basically selfish. Each individual is seen as a distinct unit whose primary concern is self-gratification. If an individual enters into positive cooperative relationships with other individuals, it will be for the sake of convenience in pursuing self-interested goals. On this view, social relationships have only an "instrumental" value.

Other philosophers view social relationships as intrinsically valuable, apart from any selfish gain involved for the participating individuals. Human beings need each other in a very basic sense. Indeed, some who have held to this view would insist that an individual who does not participate in positive social relationships is not yet "human."

A biblical given that seems to bear on this issue is God's announcement of his decision to create the woman: "It is not good that the man should be alone; I will make a helper fit for him" (Gen. 2:18).[1] Of course, both of the philosophical schools of thought mentioned above hold that it is good for individuals to participate in positive social relationships; where they disagree is over the question of *why* it is. The biblical reference we have cited does not by itself settle this question. But in its context it seems to rule out decisively— as we shall see—the view that Eve was created for Adam's "convenience."

Pursuing his decision to provide the man with a partner, the Creator brings all the animals into the man's presence. The man, in response, gives each animal a name—"but . . . there was not found a helper fit for him" (Gen. 2:20). However, when God creates the woman and brings her to the man, Adam cries out: " 'This at last is bone of my bones and flesh of my flesh' . . . and the man and his wife were both naked, and were not ashamed" (2:23, 25).

The "At last!" of the man seems to be a cry of uninhibited delight at finding someone else—neither a sovereign God nor a lowly animal, but "flesh of my flesh"—with whom to share in the business of being human. Their lack of shame at their mutual nakedness seems to suggest that there is no suspicion between them, no fear of vulnerability to mar their relationship.[2]

It must be admitted that we are dealing here with a rather meager basis for theoretical speculation. But some recent discussions of another Genesis passage seem to put the discussion on firmer ground. The passage in question is Genesis 1:26-27: "Then God said, 'Let us make man in our image, after our likeness.' . . . So God created man in his own image, in the image of God created he them."

These references to the "image of God" have been much discussed by theologians. Even though we cannot (and need

[1]Unless otherwise noted, all biblical quotations are from the Revised Standard Version.

[2]For an interesting way of distinguishing between being "unashamed" and being "shameless," with reference to this passage, see Vernard Eller, *King Jesus' Manual of Arms for the 'Armless: War and Peace from Genesis to Revelation* (Nashville: Abingdon, 1973), p. 21.

**23**

not) do justice here to the complexity of that discussion, let us review some of its main points. Two human attributes have traditionally been singled out as likely explanations for the meaning of the reference to God's "image."[3] Some have held that human beings exhibit God's image in their exercise of *rational* capacities; others have viewed humans as resembling God in the possession of a *spiritual* dimension in their makeup. Neither of these suggestions is particularly popular today, at least among theologians. A common complaint is that such traditional interpretations impose an alien philosophical framework onto the biblical account.

More recent theological discussions of the image of God reference attempt to focus on this passage without needlessly relying on extrabiblical concepts. Out of this attempt two further candidates have emerged: some theologians understand the image to consist in the *social* dimensions of human nature; while others relate it to the *office* to which the human pair was assigned with respect to the rest of creation. Since both of these topics are relevant to our present concerns, we will briefly examine the arguments offered as support for each possible interpretation.

The case for a link between the image reference and human sociality has been formulated by Karl Barth, who offers two textual considerations in support of his interpretation.[4] The first consideration is that the reference to the image is preceded by the use of plural pronouns in referring to the deity: "Let *us* make man in *our* image, after *our* likeness." This "divine plural," Barth insists, cannot be dismissed as a mere note of respect for the dignity of God; nor can we understand it as relating to a nondivine, possibly angelic, audience (a "celestial entourage") to whom God is speak-

---

[3]Extensive and helpful surveys of traditional and recent interpretations of the *imago dei* are provided by David Cairns, *The Image of God in Man* (London: Fontana, 1973), and G. C. Berkouwer, *Man: The Image of God* (Grand Rapids: Eerdmans, 1962).

[4]*Church Dogmatics*, III/1 (Edinburgh: T. & T. Clark, 1958), 183-206.

ing. The pronouns refer to a plurality *within* the deity himself.[5]

This is not to say that what we have here is an explicit, conscious reference to the Trinity, as many in the early church thought. But it is not unfair to the text, Barth argues, to see this use of the plural pronoun as a reference to "a concert of mind and act and action in the divine being itself," which pictures God as "the one and only God, yet who is not for that reason solitary, but includes in Himself the differentiation and relationship of I and Thou."[6]

Barth's second consideration is that the reference to the creation of humans in God's image is followed immediately by a reference to their being "male and female"—an indication that there is a "simple correspondence . . . between this mark of the divine being, namely, that it includes an I and a Thou, and the being of man, male and female."

Having stated his case, Barth complains:

> Is it not astonishing that again and again expositors have ignored the definitive explanation given by the text itself, and instead of reflecting on it pursued all kinds of arbitrarily invented interpretations of the *imago Dei?*—the more so when we remember that there is a detailed repetition of the Biblical explanation in Gen. 5:1: "In the day that God created man, in the likeness of God made he him; male and female created he them." Could anything be more obvious than to conclude from this clear indication that the image and likeness of the being created by God signifies existence in confrontation, i.e., in this confrontation, in the juxtaposition and conjunction of man and man which is that of male and female . . . ?[7]

Barth's confidence that he has found the "definitive" and "obvious" interpretation is, however, open to serious challenge. If we take the image to denote a respect in which humans resemble God and differ from other created beings,

[5]*Ibid.*, p. 192.
[6]*Ibid.*
[7]*Ibid.*, p. 195.

it is not at all clear that Barth's proposal is satisfactory. It is not immediately clear that being "male and female" is a way of resembling God; nor does this characteristic provide us with an unambiguous means for distinguishing humans from many animals who, from all appearances, participate in heterosexual relationships.

If Barth's account is to be salvaged from this line of criticism, some additional steps have to be taken. First, one could argue for some sort of "androgynous" deity—although it might be difficult to locate this perspective within the intentions of the biblical writer. Second, one could interpret the human male and female relationship as a special kind of "I and thou" relationship. This is Barth's actual tactic—he moves very freely between the two notions. This has the advantage of providing an understanding of "male and female" that both links humans to God and disassociates them from the animals. Its disadvantage is that it reduces the impact of Barth's claim to have found "the definitive explanation given by the text itself."

Because Barth's explanation can only be defended by considerable theorizing about the male and female reference, others have looked elsewhere in the context of the image reference for a plausible interpretation. In Genesis 1, there is also a description of the office to which the human pair was assigned: "Be fruitful and multiply, and fill the earth and subdue it; and have dominion over the fish . . . and the birds . . . and every livng thing" (vs. 28). What is significant about *this* feature—the "dominion" assignment —is that it is stressed in Psalm 8:4-8 in the context of a recitation of the significance of human createdness:

> What is man that thou art mindful of him, and the son of
> man that thou dost care for him?
> Yet thou hast made him little less than God, and dost
> crown him with glory and honor.
> Thou hast given him dominion over the work of thy hands;
> thou hast put all things under his feet . . . .

Significantly, there is no reference here to the "male and female" dimension of human nature. At the very least this counters Barth's appeal to the later reference in Genesis 5 which, when it refers to the creation of human beings, does cite their creation as "male and female."

But it does not seem that the "dominion" hypothesis can be firmly established either.[8] The phrase "little less than God" in Psalm 8 does not lend itself easily to being interpreted as another way of referring to the image of God.[9] And even if it did, we would not be left with a well-established interpretation of the reference to the image, but merely with a reasonable alternative to the "male and female" hypothesis.

Some comments might help cut through the difficult issues involved here. First, we ought not to ignore the possibility that "image of God" refers to something more complex than any of the simple hypotheses we have mentioned. This may be what Harry Kuitert has in mind when he writes:

> To look like God, to be His image, is not something we can do simply by being rational creatures or by having a good will. We cannot see God in man while man stands still. To look like God has to do with the purpose God has for man. The question, then, is what is man for, what is his calling? What is he here for? He is here to reflect God, to reflect God the Covenant Partner. To be God's image means simply that we as men are to live as covenant partners with God and with our fellows on earth.[10]

The notion of covenant-partnership might well be thought of as combining the emphasis on dominion with that of sociality: we are called to work together (sociality) in a task (dominion).

Second, even if we cannot decide with certainty in

[8]For further discussion of this hypothesis, cf. Berkouwer, *op. cit.*, pp. 70-71, and Cairns, *op. cit.*, p. 28.

[9]Cf. Berkouwer, *op. cit.*, p. 71 n. 13, for references to critical discussions of this matter.

[10]*Signals from the Bible* (Grand Rapids: Eerdmans, 1972), p. 32.

favor of any exact analysis of what the image of God consists in, we can still learn much from the attempts, even if unsuccessful, to account for it. At least this much is clear: Genesis 1 and 5 and Psalm 8 teach us that the concepts of sociality and dominion play a central role in God's creative will for human beings, whether or not those concepts have anything to do with what is referred to by the phrase "the image of God." Even G. C. Berkouwer, who seems to be skeptical about the attempts by Barth and others to give a clear account of the image of God, admits that when the New Testament speaks of the restoration of what was lost at the fall, there is a crucial emphasis on social relationships:

> It is certainly not coincidental that the calling to the imitation of God constantly concentrates on communion with others, a communion which finds its basis in the imperative reminder ". . . even as God," and ". . . even as Christ."[11]

There seem to be good reasons, then, for viewing social relationships as a central dimension of human nature from a biblical perspective. Expanding on the notion of covenant-partnership, we might put the matter this way: human beings were created for positive social cooperation with each other, to perform certain tasks with respect to the rest of creation, in obedience to the will of the Creator. It is not just that human beings were created to be social, but that they were meant to be social in certain *ways*. Their sociality was to take the form of cooperation in a task, that of having dominion, in accordance with God's will. And in obediently pursuing this social task, it is perhaps not implausible to think that human creatures are reflecting the very life of God, a point expressed well by Roch Kereszty, in the context of a criticism of the recent radical theologians:

> All the radical theologians, each in his own way, attempt to develop a community ethics as a starting point for a new humanism. But, they all reject God as not only irrele-

[11]*Op. cit.*, p. 115.

vant to, but actually obstructive of, such ethics. They all conceive of God as a solitary powerful Lord. . . . They do not even seem to know about the Christian mystery of the Trinity. . . . God is not, as it were, an isolated kingly hermit, but an infinitely powerful and intense communication of life between the Father and the Son in the Spirit. . . . The Triune God is the model of perfect community that makes us understand why a human person becomes truly himself only if he is integrated into a community.
. . . The central Christian mystery, if presented in the "language" of our times is perhaps more "relevant" than ever before. The total self-giving of God to man in Christ that constitutes the infinite value of the human person, the Trinitarian communion as the archetype, source, and ultimate assurance of every human communion, corresponds to the most pressing needs and hopes of modern man.[12]

# CREATED SOCIALITY

In the story of the Garden we have a glimpse of the human social condition as the Creator intended it to be. What are the implications of this picture for our further reflections on the place of political patterns in the biblical drama? A discussion of created sociality is important for the other issues that we must face. Questions about the origin and ground of political structures cannot be dealt with adequately unless we have some notion of the patterns of sociality they are meant to expedite. Views about which political structures are best for human beings presuppose a prior opinion as to the *point* of those structures. In order to be clear about the implications of what we have established thus far, several comments are in order.

First, the creation account rules out acceptance by Christians of any theory that views positive social arrangements as an unnatural imposition on human nature. Specifically, it rules out the Hobbesian conception of an original

[12]*God-Seekers for a New Age* (Dayton, Ohio: Pflaum Press, 1970), pp. 135f.

"state of nature" in which self-centered human beings are in a state of "war"—a condition superseded by the relative "peace" made possible by the establishment of a coercive state. From a biblical point of view, the "original" condition is one of peace and harmony.

This is not to say that a Christian cannot legitimately picture the *fallen* condition in terms similar to the Hobbesian state of nature. It may be that human rebellion manifests itself in the kind of self-centeredness which Hobbes viewed as natural for human beings. What is excluded by the Genesis story is the proposal that the condition of war is the normal state of affairs for humans.

Second, while the Genesis account rules out a thorough-going individualism, it also suggests that we ought to resist those views of human sociality which tend completely to absorb individuals into the larger social unit. The individuals who are created for social relationships are nonetheless *individuals*. Indeed, the Bible pictures sociality as being central to created human nature, but that sociality is not exhausted by *human* social relationships: the human pair is created to engage in a common life *before God*.

This two-directional sociality is also stressed in the New Testament's call to love both God and neighbor. It is important to keep both the distinctions and the similarities between these two directions in mind. The Westminster Catechism tells us that "the chief end of man is to glorify God"—an important reminder that human relationships and activities are not "self-contained" but must be viewed in the light of the Creator's will—but the Catechism adds that by glorifying God we "enjoy him forever." We are to glorify God in our human relationships in order to bring him honor. But what do God's glory and honor consist in? God's own "well-being" must not be pictured in terms of that of a selfish despot who revels in his ability to manipulate us. Rather, it is the glory of a benevolent Creator who desires to reveal his love in and through our lives. God is properly honored when his peace, his *Shalom*, is manifested within his creation. We obey God for *his* sake; but his "sake" consists in his desire that we "enjoy him forever" by being perfected and fulfilled in accordance with his creating purposes.

Third, the capacity for social relationships with which humans are created can be exercised either positively or negatively. Here, too, we must mention those views which tend to absorb individuals into the larger social unit. Arguments for this kind of perspective often rely heavily on metaphors which liken relationships between human beings to the relationships that hold between bodily parts. This analogy is not illegitimate, so long as the analogous nature of the comparison is kept in view. Indeed, St. Paul uses this very analogy in discussing the relationships that ought to characterize the Christian community: "For just as in a single body there are many limbs and organs, all with different functions, so all of us, united with Christ, form one body, serving individually as limbs and organs to one another" (Rom. 12:4-5, NEB). But, as F. W. Dillistone puts it, Paul's use of "organism" language here must be interpreted, not "metaphysically and mystically," but "metaphorically and ethically."[13]

Human beings, like parts of a body, depend on each other; they need each other. But the *ways* in which human individuals are interdependent is not the same as the mutual dependency of bodily parts. The latter are physically and organically interdependent; human beings are *socially* interdependent. There is no future for a hand that becomes separated from the body of which it is an organic part. There is no *good* future—although there may be a future—for an individual who becomes separated from harmonious social relationships.

The possibility of sin rests on this point: it was not *impossible* for human beings to rebel against God and against each other; it was *wrong*. The death forecast as a result of sin was not physical death but moral and social death. Indeed, the Bible pictures hell not as the annihilation of the individual, but as a condition in which every sem-

[13]*The Structure of the Divine Society* (Philadelphia: Westminster, 1951), p. 181.

blance of sociality is finally eliminated and the individual is alone, weeping, wailing, and gnashing his teeth.

Finally, there is nothing in the creation account to indicate a natural hierarchy among humans. There is a hierarchy that requires the human pair to submit together to the will of God, and in turn to have dominion over the animals; but there is no suggestion that one of them is thought to be subordinate to the other (unless we speculate—questionably—that Adam's willingness to follow Eve in eating the forbidden fruit was a part of an established pattern on his part). There was, we conclude, no coercive "sexual politics" in the Garden.

The question of "subordination" is raised only after the curse of sin comes into effect. No matter how we interpret later references to a required "submission" on the part of the woman (see I Tim. 2:11), the Genesis account gives us no reason to think that it was a part of the original plan for creation. It is also significant that there is no reference to this kind of patriarchy in the establishment of the "rule of the saints" in the future age, when "there shall no more be anything accursed" (Rev. 22:3-4). We will suggest later that some kind of hierarchy might have evolved if sin had not entered the situation; but there is no reason to think that such a hierarchical pattern among humans would be based on patriarchy or any other allegedly natural structure.

## CREATED POLITICS?

Was there anything in the unfallen creation which could be properly described as a political order?

A negative answer to that question has been defended by Gordon Clark. Before the fall, he argues, "there was no provision for civil government";[14] government and politics are essentially matters of coercion, an element that is necessarily introduced into human affairs when there is "a large number of evil people working at cross purposes."[15] Coer-

[14]A Christian View of Men and Things (Grand Rapids: Eerdmans, 1952), p. 138.
[15]Ibid., p. 146.

cion was not necessary in the Garden, however; hence there was no need for politics. Government is only necessary when "sinful man needs to be restrained, and it is in connection with man's acquired evil nature that the ideas of master, servant, and ruler enter."[16]

At first glance this might seem to be an attractive—indeed a commonsensical—position. But reflecting on it, we are led to ask some questions. First, while Clark is correct that there was no *civil* government in the Garden, it is not clear that the concept of *government* as such is inapplicable to the situation. Indeed, it would not be absurd to describe the small community in the Garden as constituting a "theocracy": God can be properly spoken of as ruling over Adam and Eve. And that Adam and Eve in turn were together given a mandate to have dominion over the animal world suggests that they too exercised a kind of rule.

Second, Clark's contention that "the ideas of master, servant, and ruler" are necessarily connected with "man's acquired evil nature" seems false. Not only is it reasonable, as we have suggested, to apply these ideas to the unfallen condition, but the New Testament employs those very concepts to describe the relationship between human beings and God in the context of both the church and the future kingdom. In Revelation 22:3-5, the announcement that "there shall no more be anything accursed" is immediately followed by references to God's "throne," the worship of God's "servants," and the "rule" of the saints.

Third—and most important—we should not confuse the claim that there was, in fact, no "civil government" in the Garden (which is correct) with Clark's stronger claim that "there was no *provision* for civil government." It is possible that the absence of civil government in the Garden was due not to the sinlessness of the situation but to the extremely small human population of the Garden. Suppose that the human race had grown in numbers even if the fall had not occurred. That civil government is not pictured as entering

[16]*Ibid.*, p. 138.

into human affairs even immediately *after* the fall into sin seems to suggest that family or tribal governments are possible alternatives to full-fledged states when large numbers of people are not yet present.

This is, roughly, the thesis of Abraham Kuyper. In one of his 1898 Stone Lectures at Princeton Seminary, Kuyper argues that without the fall there would have nonetheless developed a political order, but along different lines from that which led to the existence of states and magistrates. "Political life in its entirety," Kuyper argues, "would have evolved itself, after a patriarchal fashion, from the life of the family."[17] He summarizes his view as follows:

> Even without sin the need would have asserted itself of combining the many families into a higher unity, but this unity would have *internally* been bound up in the Kingship of God, which would have ruled regularly, directly and harmoniously in the hearts of all men, and which would *externally* have incorporated itself in a patriarchial hierarchy. Thus, no States would have existed, but only one organic world-empire, with God as its King; exactly what is prophesied for the future which awaits us, when all sin shall have disappeared.
>
> But it is exactly this, which sin has now eliminated from our human life. This unity does not any longer exist. . . . Thus peoples and nations originated. These peoples formed States. And over these States God appointed *governments*. And thus, if I may be allowed the expression, it is not a natural head, which organically grew from the body of the people, but a *mechanical* head, which from without has been placed upon the trunk of the nation. A mere remedy, therefore, for a wrong condition supervening. A stick placed beside the plant to hold it up, since without it, by reason of its inherent weakness, it would fall to the ground.[18]

Kuyper's view is not without defects. For one thing,

[17] Abraham Kuyper, *Lectures on Calvinism* (Grand Rapids: Eerdmans, 1931), p. 80.
[18] *Ibid.*, pp. 92f.

why does he insist that the basic authority-structures of the family must be patriarchial in form, since—as was indicated earlier—there is no hint of a hierarchical system before the fall? Furthermore, since he does allow for at least two levels of authority-patterns under sinless conditions—first, the authority-patterns *within* the individual family; and, second, the grouping together of families under the rule of God—it could be asked why there could not be intermediate groupings—say, some families coming together for a pooling of resources under a common decision-making procedure, which would allow for political structures that functioned between the rule of God and the rule of the basic family unit.

However, taken as a general sort of proposal, this position seems more plausible than Clark's. We must emphasize that the differences between these two positions are not merely "semantic." For Clark civil government as we presently experience it is purely negative or remedial in function, nothing more than a means of guarding against the excessive selfishness associated with the sinful condition. On Kuyper's view, however, the political order—while presently having these remedial functions—also makes a positive contribution to human social life, a contribution it might have to make even if sin were not a part of the picture.

The disagreements on this level become crucial ones, as we shall see when we consider the question of whether it is legitimate for a Christian to participate in government activities. The issue then becomes: are the patterns of domination and manipulation that presently characterize political activity to be understood as the *essential* properties of an order introduced into creation as a result of sin or do they constitute a *perversion* of an order that was a part of the original creation?

The former view—government as essentially "coercive" —is an important element in John Howard Yoder's argument that Christians ought not to participate in government. Yoder writes:

It is not as if there was a time when there was no govern-

ment and then God made government through a new creative intervention; there has been hierarchy and authority
and power since human society existed. Its exercise has
involved domination, disrespect for human dignity, and
real or potential violence ever since sin has existed.[19]

We can agree with this comment as it stands, since it suggests that there is a legitimate distinction between sinful
society and "human society" as such. But since Yoder seems
to want to allow for a wedge here between a society characterized by "hierarchy and authority and power" and one
involving "domination, disrespect for human dignity, and
real or potential violence," it is difficult to understand why
Yoder denies—as we will see in a later chapter—that there
are criteria we can employ in the political arena to distinguish between just and unjust governments.

To expand on a suggestion made earlier, suppose that
even without the entrance of sin into their lives Adam and
Eve had been obedient to the command to "be fruitful
and multiply," with the result that there came to be a
rather large number of unfallen human beings. Why could
there not be in such a society a body of appointed representatives who functioned, roughly, between God and the
humans they represented? (To imagine this, we do not
have to introduce the kind of hierarchy we earlier rejected;
appointment to such a function might be open to everyone
on a rotating basis.) Perhaps it would be the job of these
representatives to make decisions in certain specified areas
—e.g., to set time schedules and to decide which side of the
road to drive on—which would require regulation even
where sin was not a part of the picture. Here there
would be some sort of "hierarchy and authority and power,"
but presumably not of the sort that would produce "domination, disrespect for human dignity, and real or potential
violence." It is in this sense that we should think of politics
as being rooted in the order of creation, and not as merely
a post-fall phenomenon.

[19]John H. Yoder, *The Politics of Jesus* (Grand Rapids: Eerdmans,
1972), p. 203.

# CHAPTER THREE

# SIN AND POLITICS

It was common for theologians of a previous generation, especially those of Reformed persuasion, to describe sin as ethical rebellion. This seems to be an apt way of putting the matter. Sin as portrayed in the Scriptures is not merely the condition of being finite, or of being aware of one's finitude, or even of being anxious in one's awareness of finitude. It is the condition of rebelling against the acceptance of one's assigned place in the creation, in such a way that one can be held responsible for that rebellion.

Sin, as pictured in the Bible, involves self-deception. The latter is a very puzzling phenomenon, but there can be no doubt that it afflicts human experience at many levels, as the existentialist philosophers have insisted. Self-deception includes two elements which, when they appear together in a single situation, constitute a strange state of affairs. First, self-deception involves deception. When we are in this condition we believe something which is not actually true. But the deception is, in the second place, self-inflicted. And just as in cases of one person's deliberately deceiving another person, we have a right to hold the deceiver responsible for the perpetration of the false-hood. In this case we are both deceived and guilty of deception.

Consider an example. Suppose a woman's husband is carrying on an extra-marital affair, and there is evidence available to her of his wrongdoing. At parties he spends considerable time in whispered conversations with the "other woman." He regularly offers weak excuses about "working late at the office," and is absent without being able to account for his time or whereabouts. In each case she either ignores the evidence or goes out of her way to provide him with "innocent" excuses for his pattern of behavior. When the possibility of unfaithfulness on his part enters her mind, or is suggested to her by someone else, she quickly dismisses the thought.

Suppose that there comes a time when she can no longer ignore the facts, and she openly acknowledges that her husband has been having an affair. If her mental condition had been a genuine case of self-deception, her acknowledgment will now include two elements. First, she will insist that she did not consciously entertain the thought that her husband was being unfaithful—she did not, in an important sense, *believe* the truth. But, secondly, she now holds herself responsible for her "ignorance" of the situation. She insists on saying of herself that she "should have known better," that she was a "fool" for not seeing the true state of affairs.

The Scriptures portray the sinful condition as a situation of this kind. When unbelievers argue against the existence of God they are not being insincere in a straight-forward manner; they consciously deny the truth of the biblical message. But they are also pictured as knowing the truth in an important sense. As the Apostle puts it, they "suppress the truth . . . they are without excuse; for although they knew God they did not honor him as God" (Rom. 1:18, 20-21).

As harsh as this analysis may seem, it fits the actual experience of persons who have become Christians. It is common for those who have come to acknowledge Christ as the Lord of their lives to insist that while there was a time when they consciously denied the truth of the gospel, they are nevertheless to be held *responsible* for that unbelief; they now insist that they were guilty of pride, even though they would have sincerely rejected that ascription at the time of their honest doubts.

This pattern of self-deception can be seen operating in the biblical account of the fall. In rebelling against the will of their Creator, Adam and Eve came to accept certain falsehoods, for which they are clearly to be held accountable. We must look more closely now at the nature of their rebellious unbelief.

## TWO SERPENTINE FALSEHOODS

The fall of the human race into sin resulted from succumbing to the Tempter's challenge: "You will be like God" (Gen. 3:5). The positive response by Eve and Adam to this challenge involved two factors relevant to our discussion. First, they accepted the serpent's doctrine of God, which we might call "revisionist" doctrine. The God against whom they were challenged to rebel was pictured as a despot whose unreasonable demands could only squelch human potential. God is pictured as a deceiver—in spite of the divine warning, the serpent reassures Eve, "you shall *not* surely die"—who is jealous of his exclusive position as the one who knows "good and evil."

This is a very common view of the biblical deity, and it is regularly presupposed in criticism of the Christian way of life. Thus, Erich Fromm can describe the fall into sin as a means for *improving* man's condition:

> Acting against God's orders means freeing himself from coercion, emerging from the unconscious existence of pre-human life to the level of man. Acting against the command of authority, committing a sin, is in its positive human aspect the first act of freedom, that is, the first

*human* act. In the myth the sin in its formal aspect is the eating of the tree of knowledge. The act of disobedience as an act of freedom is the beginning of reason.[1]

If we assume the serpentine conception of God, we might well agree with Fromm and others, who view rebellion against the Creator as an act of "growing up." It is not especially sinful to refuse to submit to the whims of bullies and despots. If it were this kind of refusal that occurred in the Garden, we might well laud Adam and Eve as having launched the first recorded campaign in favor of "maturity," or even democracy.

In fact we do not always praise the pattern of rebellion Fromm describes as a noble event. We do not look with approval on the three-year-old child who disobediently persists in running into busy thoroughfares. Nor do we always applaud escapes from prison or attempts at assassination. To cite these examples does not suggest favorable comparisons between the unfallen condition and infancy or imprisonment, but merely insists that the merits of a rebellious act cannot be considered apart from an evaluation of the object of that rebellion. To put it simply, if God *was* a deceptive despot, Adam and Eve had a right to rebel; but if the serpentine accusation was unfair, their rebellion was not legitimate.

The biblical account gives us no reason for assuming that the Tempter's challenge was a fair representation of God's intentions. Indeed, we are given considerable evidence against this view. The Creator had spoken with affection when he had originally noted the loneliness of the man. And this affection does not completely disappear, even after their rebellion. Quite the contrary. The whole remainder of the story is given over to an elaborate attempt to rescue humans from the otherwise inevitable death of their rebellion, until finally the Creator can proclaim "Behold, I make all things new," while wiping the tears from human eyes (see Rev. 21:4-5).

[1]*Escape from Freedom* (New York: Avon Books, 1941), p. 50.

Most important, however, is the fact that the story of the reclamation of fallen humanity directly confronts the revisionist doctrine of God that precipitated the fall into sin. Over and over, human beings must hear the refrain, "You have misunderstood; *that* is not what it means to be a 'lord.'" Finally God himself must become a member of sinful humanity, so that human beings can once again cry out in surprised joy: "At last! Flesh of my flesh and bone of my bone!" "The Word became flesh and dwelt among us, full of grace and truth" (John 1:14). The lie of the Tempter is decisively exposed when the incarnate Son says, "Look! *This* is what it means to be a 'lord'": and "he emptied himself, taking the form of a servant . . . and became obedient unto death, even death on a cross" (Phil. 2:27-28).

The second factor involved in the sin of the fall is that Adam and Eve initiated a project by which they attempted to *conform* to this false model of what a deity is: "*You* will be as God." Here we can see an important facet of John Calvin's insistence, in the opening pages of his *Institutes,* that the knowledge of God and the knowledge of self are inseparable. A change in human perspectives on the nature and motives of the Creator immediately signaled a change in self-image. Having revised their concept of "lordship" from the idea of a loving creator to that of a selfish despot, Adam and Eve aspired to this latter kind of lordship.

## SIN AND SELFISHNESS

There are important connections between the condition of sin and human patterns of selfish manipulation. In order better to understand these connections we must investigate the relationship between sin and selfishness, and between sin and the desire to manipulate others.

Philosophers have rightly distinguished between two theses about the alleged role of selfishness in human activity. *Psychological egoism* is a theory about the actual motivations operating in human decision-making. According to this perspective each human action is in fact motivated by a desire for selfish gain. *Normative egoism* is a theory about how human beings ought to act. It is in effect a proposal that people ought to be motivated by a desire for selfish gain.

These two theses are logically distinct. One might believe that people are selfish but that they ought *not* to be. Or one could believe that human beings ought to be selfish and yet admit that on many occasions people are not in fact so motivated. We will limit our attention here to the psychological or descriptive thesis, briefly commenting on the relationship between this thesis and the Christian belief that human beings are sinful. We cannot explore all of the criticisms lodged against psychological egoism, but two of the most common ones deserve mention.

First, it is often charged that the claim that all human acts are selfishly motivated is usually defended in such a way that it is difficult even to conceive of an act that the proponent of psychological egoism would admit as an "unselfish" one. Defenders of psychological egoism do not usually state their theory in a way that would help predict which among several courses of action a given agent would choose. Rather, the theory serves as a basis for explaining the way in which *whatever* action is chosen can be seen as a "selfish" one. Thus, if a mother refuses to rescue her child from a burning house, she is viewed as selfishly protecting her own life; but if she does attempt to rescue her child, she is described as selfishly satisfying a "maternal instinct."

Second, the psychological egoist is often accused of failing to make some important distinctions, for example, that between the "motivation" of an act and the "object" of the same act. In the situation just cited, the mother attempts in the one case to protect her own life without showing a concern for that of the child; while in the other, she is willing to risk her own well-being for the sake of the child's safety. Even if it could be argued plausibly that there was a selfish motive present in both cases, there is an important difference between the two courses of action: in the one she "selfishly" saves her own life, while in the other she "selfishly" saves the life of the child. Even though we might for the sake of the argument allow both cases to be viewed as selfish, the different ways in which that selfishness is pursued in each case—that is, the different objects (mother's safety, child's safety) of the actions— still seem to require us to make some kind of further distinction between "selfish" and "unselfish" actions.

Christians have seldom been inclined to hold to a straightforward version of psychological egoism. For one thing most Christians have automatically excluded the actions of God and of the incarnate Jesus from the realm of selfish activity. Furthermore, most Christians would acknowledge actual cases of unselfish acts on a purely human level—such as actions similar to the behavior of the Good Samaritan, as well as the sacrificial deeds of the martyrs.

What some Christians have done, however, is to identify sinful actions as selfish ones, so that to the degree to which an action can be considered sinful, it is selfish. This has characterized certain strands of liberal theology, which view the self-sacrificial death of Jesus as an antidote—by way of providing an "example" of unselfishness—to our natural tendencies toward selfishness. It has also, interestingly enough, characterized some fundamentalist thought, especially that which defends the capitalist system on the ground that "we are all selfish anyway." (It is not uncommon to hear fundamentalists say that socialism might work in heaven, but not here on earth.)

The problems with trying to interpret sinful activity as selfish in nature are not much different from the problems associated with the doctrine of psychological egoism as such. It just does not seem very useful to describe all sinful activity as selfish, in the light of the fact that much of that activity *seems* to be unselfish. It begins to look as though the only way of rescuing the thesis is by holding that not all *seemingly* sinful actions are actually sinful. Furthermore, it would also seem necessary to introduce the "motive"/"object" distinction with respect to sinful activity.

In what sense, then, can we link sin and selfishness? Here we should note the important sense in which we can formulate a doctrine of sin without referring to selfishness at all. There is no reason why we have to understand the Tempter's challenge "You shall be as God" as "You will serve only yourself." It is more accurate to view sin, not simply as a love of *self*, but as a love of the creaturely. This is why the distinction between Creator and creation is such a fundamental one in Christian thought. The Bible warns us against the idolatry that characterizes the sinful state. Sin results from misplacing the trust that rightly resides in the love of God in some dimension of his creation.

Straightforward love of self—ordinarily called egotism— is only one way of loving the creaturely. When human beings pursue idolatrous patterns of life, there is a large variety of potential candidates for their idolatrous trust, and the majority of these candidates have been elected at one time or another. Some have worshiped, as in St. Paul's account, "images resembling mortal man or birds or animals or reptiles" (Rom. 1:23). But others have placed their ultimate hope in economic systems or political ideologies, sexual satisfaction, aesthetic enjoyment, and the like. Straightforward love of self is not obviously common to all of these patterns of devotion; for this reason, it is proper to describe some sinners as "selfish" and others as "altruistic."

But there is also a significant sense in which we can say that sin is based on selfishness, just as long as we do not confuse this view with the thesis of psychological egoism. Not every sinful act is a selfish one—the kamikazi pilots' devotion to the Emperor seems to have been idolatrous, but not very selfish in nature. But the patterns of idolatry that we choose to pursue do stem from a selfish attitude, namely, one of pride. This pride leads us into some curious situations. In our rebellion against the Creator, we are willing even to bow and scrape before brutal dictators and dumb idols— in effect, before anything but the true God. Because we are willing to bow and scrape, it is wrong to describe all of our actions as "selfish"; but because we are willing to trust in anything but the Creator, our attitudes can be rightly viewed as stemming from "selfish pride."

Even though we will not be discussing the desirability of specific forms of government, an implication of what we have been arguing here should be obvious: there is no biblical basis for defending the capitalist system or for criticizing socialist theories of government on the ground that human beings are selfish. It is a fact that sinful human beings have manifested an enormous capacity for self-sacrificial devotion to specific political and economic systems. The fact that this capacity exists should not be surprising from a biblical perspective. Nor is there any reason to commend these patterns of altruism on biblical grounds. In each case, the Christian critique must focus on the question of where ultimate loyalty and hope reside. When we sing that "the arm of flesh will fail us," we should understand this as referring to both capitalist flesh and socialist flesh—and even "mixed economy" flesh—when those systems are portrayed to us as means of redemption.

## SIN AND MANIPULATION

Any attempt at a link between sin and manipulation must also be qualified in significant respects. But before introducing the necessary qualifications we will consider the connection in its unqualified form.

One result of sin in the biblical account is that human beings begin to view each other with suspicion and distrust —as one would expect from persons who have succumbed to the despotic model of deity. The relationship between the man and the woman now includes grudging services performed in sweat and pain (Gen. 3:16-19). The serpent, once a creature over whom they had been given dominion, now becomes a cursed and cursing thing in their eyes; the way is now open for the development of patterns of domination.

"Management" and "control" now become prized commodities in human relationships. Where there was once spontaneous trust and commitment between the man and the woman, their mutual nakedness now becomes an occasion for vulnerability—something which must be considered a risk in a relationship between "gods."

It is not surprising that in this kind of situation the sexual relationship—to consider one example—should take on dimensions different from those which might characterize a sinless state of affairs. Consider these observations by Seymour Halleck on the subtleties of the sexual relationship:

> Sex can be used to relieve tensions, to gain status, to obtain reassurance, to flatter one's vanity, to express love, and to gain a certain amount of control over the behavior of others. In short it is not only a loving act but can also be used as a vehicle for establishing one's sense of power. . . . [This] suggests that the bedroom, in addition to being a place for the expression of tenderness toward another human being, can also be an arena or battlefield in which the participants are striving to strengthen their position in a social system.[2]

If the goal of sexual activity is simply the expression of love and affection between two trusting persons, tender and spontaneous gestures can occur. But these become more difficult to achieve when sexuality is characterized by the factors described by Halleck; here spontaneity and tenderness can become subordinate to other goals. The sexual partner must now ask: How can I stay in "control"? What must I do in order to maintain a "bargaining" position? The fall into sin can be viewed as involving a shift toward these kinds of "management" relations on an interpersonal level.

Similar patterns came to be manifested on a more institutionalized level also, as can be seen by using Paul Goodman's distinction between "normal" and "neurotic" institutional patterns.[3] In a normal institution, the decision-making

[2]Seymour Halleck, "Sex and Power," in *Medical Aspects of Human Sexuality* (October 1969).
[3]*People or Personnel* (New York: Random House, 1963), pp. 183f.

patterns and the tools for expediting the institutional functions—in short, the "politics" and the "technology"—are viewed as mere means for achieving certain desired social goals. In a neurotic institution, the maintenance of the politics and technology itself becomes the goal of institutional activity.

Consider an example. Libraries came into being, presumably, for a rather simple reason: to make it easier for people to have access to books. In what we might call a normal library, the rules, regulations, technology, and so on would be directed toward the goal of providing relatively uncomplicated means for books to circulate among readers. Library cards, systems of classification, neat rows of books on serviceable shelves, procedures regulating the traffic of books—all of these things would be directed toward that goal.

On occasion, however, the maintenance of such things becomes a goal in itself, so that a library comes to have as its primary goals the collection, classification, and storage of books. Under these conditions, the potential borrower, the reader of books—for whom the institution was set up in the first place—becomes an enemy, a threat to the maintenance of neat rows of books on tidy shelves. What we have, then, is a neurotic library, one in which the well-being of what were once the intended beneficiaries becomes detrimental to the new goal of managing the institutional structures.

In neurotic situations, whether on the personal or institutional level, the management of the politics and technology becomes the goal, and the meeting of human needs and desires, originally the proper goal of the arrangement, becomes a secondary consideration. To borrow Martin Buber's terminology, both a sexual relationship and a library can conceivably be occasions for realizing "I-thou" relationships: sexual partners can relate to each other affectionately and spontaneously, and libraries can provide a context in which one group provides another with the access to books. But on each level it is also possible for some or all of the parties involved to become "objects" to be manipulated for the sake of managing either the relationship or the institution. When this happens we have what is commonly referred to as dehumanization.

Christianity itself can be an occasion for realizing neurotic patterns. The most common case of this is "legalism," in which the person's relationship to God deteriorates into a rigid submission to God's commandments. The result is that the law becomes a thing-to-be-obeyed, the individual adopts the role of law-obeyer, and the management of this relationship between the commandment and the one commanded becomes a matter of primary importance. What is lost in such a situation is the dimension of spontaneous—even affectionate ("Abba, Father")—love between persons that ought to characterize covenant partnership.

To realize that legalism is a distortion of the appropriate relationship between the Creator and his human creatures, is to recognize that the relation between persons—in this case, a divine person and a human one—is of primary value. Indeed, it is the distortion of this relationship which brings about the perversion of all the rest, according to the biblical picture. When the spontaneous love of God becomes impossible, spontaneous relationships become difficult all along the way. Even the alleged spontaneity of the sexual orgy often becomes dominated by a concern for technique.

## SINFUL POLITICS

In raising the question of the relationship between sin and manipulative activity, we have only touched on an immense and complicated topic. Our main purpose in raising the question at all is to gain some understanding of the ways, not always borne in mind in the past, sin has influenced our social and political patterns of behavior. We must now add some further clarifying and qualifying observations, however, in order to avoid some misunderstandings.

First, it would be misleading to link sin with the desire to manipulate as such without pointing out that the condition of being manipulated can also be a manifestation of sinful rebellion. If adopting the role of a coercive "lord" is an expression of sin, so is viewing oneself merely as an object to be manipulated by other "lords." To point this out is not to refuse sympathy toward oppressed peoples; but we ought to be at least sensitive to the suggestion of Jean-Paul Sartre and others, that masochism as well as sadism can be a pattern of "bad faith." Whether we view ourselves as manipulators or objects to be manipulated, we are understanding ourselves as less than the creatures that we are meant to be.

Indeed, it is unlikely that there have been many human beings who have simply been oppressed without also engaging in oppression of their own. White middle-class American women who are oppressed by their husbands are often very racist in their attitudes toward the poor. Black male slaves often treated women slaves as sex-objects. Women slaves have, on occasion, been cruel to their children. And so on. The patterns of human manipulation are subtly interwoven.

Second, the "systemic" manipulation that we discussed with reference to libraries must be viewed as both related to and distinguishable from very personal patterns of oppression. The two are related in that the Bible pictures all injustice and oppression as stemming from a posture of personal rebellion against the Creator. Corporate injustice and the neurotic patterns that characterize collective interaction are results of the institutionalization of this personal rebellion. The collective technological experiment at Babel, where human beings attempted to build "a tower with its top in the heavens" (Gen. 11:4), was a corporate project which embodied the desire to be as God. This same kind of embodiment can take place in marital, economic, and political patterns.

But these institutionalizations of the personal sinful project can come to have a life of their own. For this reason it is not enough to insist, as many conservative evangelical Christians have done, that "changed hearts will change society." If the manipulative patterns which are built into the very structures of social relationships are not changed, all of the effects of sin have not been challenged—and it may be that as a result many "hearts" will not be capable of adequate "change."

Third, what the biblical perspective offers is a framework within which we can see the "beyond," or the "transcendent residue," of all human personal and institutional relationships. The Bible tells us that we are responsible creatures of God, called to a loving partnership with him. An important dimension of this fellowship with the Creator is a resultant attitude of self-assessment. In the light of this relationship we can pray: "Search me, O God, and know my heart! Try me and know my thoughts! And see if there be any wicked way in me, and lead me in the way everlasting" (Ps. 139:23-24), thus opening up all of our intentions, roles, and involvements to divine scrutiny.

A fourth observation is closely related to this. Strictly speaking, "dehumanization" is impossible. We cannot become *less* than the responsible persons who are called to covenant partnership with God and our fellow humans. As much as we attempt to define ourselves in terms of any lesser role, we will fail. This is why it is important not to restrict the application of the term "oppression" to *inter*personal relationships; there is also a kind of oppression that we experience in the "intra-personal" attempt to conform to something that we are not—namely, something less than the children of God.

Fifth, we must also note that institutional or corporate oppression can take many different forms. There is the oppression that is experienced in the context of clumsy bureaucracies, in which every person is subsumed under an institutional role—the domain of the "Peter Principle"—and no one is happy. There is also the oppression experienced when a given institution is the creation or expression of the will of a powerful individual or group, so that a structured tyranny exists to satisfy the selfish desires of a few. There are also those situations in which a given institution serves as the medium for exchange between two or more powerful groups at the expense of a large number of others who are affected by the life of the institution: for example, in a government controlled by a military-industrial complex primary value is placed on power-brokering between politicians and military-industrial types, at the expense of suffering on the part of the vast majority of the citizenry.

Finally, we must insist that nothing in our account is meant to indicate that "roles," institutional "machinery," decision-making procedures, and the like are bad *as such*. We have referred favorably in our discussion to spontaneous relationships, but there is no reason to think that we are obligated to *maximize* spontaneity. As we have already indicated, standardized decision-making procedures and a certain amount of "role-playing" might be appropriate in a *sinless* state of affairs. Even the honesty and openness cherished by those who have received "sensitivity training" are not always desirable elements in human relationships. What seems to be required of us is that we, first of all, be the kind of persons who are capable of honesty, openness, and spontaneity, and secondly, that we cultivate those characteristics on a regular basis. Equipped with those sensitivities, we can then enter into roles and procedures on occasion with attitudes of self-awareness and even humor, because we know that we are *more* than the situation by itself would indicate.

The most systematic defense of "de-politicizing" human relationships can be found in Marxist writings. But even there we often find indications that Marxists are incapable of imagining a totally spontaneous, "unmanaged" society. When Leon Trotsky denounced the post-revolutionary Soviet government as "a bureaucratic-Bonapartist regime of insufferable harshness, arbitrariness and rottenness," he observed that

A society whose socialist structure is assured, whose internal relations thus repose upon the solidarity of the overwhelming mass, does not require an internal dictatorship for protection from external foes but only a technico-military apparatus, just as it requires a technico-economic apparatus for its welfare.[4]

And Engels describes the process of the "withering-away of the State" in this way:

> State interference in social relations becomes, in one domain after another, superfluous, and then dies out of itself; the government of persons is replaced by the administration of things, and by the conduct of processes of production.[5]

It is not obstinate to ask whether what is being pictured in each of these comments is not a residual "government" of an important sort: neither a "technico-military apparatus," nor a "technico-economic apparatus," nor "the conduct of processes of production" can exist for long without standardized procedures and a set of assigned roles.

## THE DIVINE RESPONSE

We now have some picture of the gap between society as it was intended by God, and the social and political ramifications of the fall. The attempted polytheism of God's fallen creatures manifests itself in a situation in which politics—both in the traditional narrow sense and the recently expanded sense of the term—becomes an occasion for manipulative projects and oppressive policies. As a result of the fall, the tragic boast "We will be like God" reverberates throughout the creation.

But the rebellious cries of God's creatures are not the final words to be heard in the drama. The God who had freely chosen to create now graciously decides to reclaim the

[4]Leon Trotsky, "Karl Kiebknect and Rosa Luxemburg: Martyrs of the Third International," *International Socialist Review* (Jan. 1971); excerpted in *Political Ideologies*, ed. J. A. Gould and W. H. Truitt (New York: Macmillan, 1973).

[5]Karl Marx and Frederick Engels, *Selected Works* (Moscow: Foreign Languages Publishing House, 1962), II, 151.

lost. In the midst of the almost-total destruction of the Flood he renews his creative intentions when he repeats the original mandate to Noah: "For God made man in his own image. And you, be fruitful and multiply, bring forth abundantly on the earth and multiply in it" (Gen. 9:6-7). And Abram, with the "we will be as God" of rebellious humanity echoing all around him, suddenly hears a new and better pledge: "I will be God to you and to your descendants after you" (Gen. 17:7).

" I will be God to you." If there were no further words that could rightly be attributed to the Creator, these alone would be "good news," for they constitute a fundamental and gracious response to the sin of the fall. In the midst of a rebellious creation God has made it possible for at least some of his human creatures to proclaim "Emmanuel, God is with us."And just as God's initial address to humanity was *as* a plurality *to* a plurality, so the work of redemption is one whereby the Triune God creates a new *people.* The social and political barriers erected by sin can now be broken down. The new community of the "people of God" constitutes the reinstatement of the social bond broken and distorted by human rebellion.

# CHAPTER FOUR

# REDEEMED SOCIETY: THE CHURCH'S LIFE AND MISSION

Questions about the nature and mission of the Christian church are crucial topics for political theological discussion. In the first place, there are fascinating parallels between ecclesiological theories and some traditional philosophical perspectives on the "ontological" makeup of societies as such. Just as some philosophers have insisted that social and political relationships are justifiably formed only for the convenience of the individual participants' pursuits of independently specifiable goals, so individualistic ecclesiologies suggest that the church is a mere "fellowship of believers," whose private, individual relationships with God are primary, but who may become "associated in a common cause which may be for convenience considered in the light of a combined result."[1] Similarly those ecclesiological emphases—especially in some strands of traditional Roman Catholicism—which rely heavily on the organic metaphors of biblical references to the church run the risk of approx-

[1]Lewis Sperry Chafer, *Systematic Theology* (Dallas: Dallas Seminary Press, 1948), IV, 149.

imating the totalitarian patterns of extreme organicist views of the political order.[2]

Second, the church occupies a central place in God's revelation of his social and political purposes for human beings. The parallels we mentioned between ecclesiology and traditional social-political perspectives are not mere coincidences. The church, on anyone's interpretation, is a social institution with patterns of authority and decision-making; if we also hold that it is intended by its very existence to be a model, even a revelation, of God's will for corporate existence, then the parallels between ecclesiology and social/political theory take on important dimensions.

Third, the doctrine of the church is an important context for discussing the ways Christians are to have an impact on the actual political processes of the larger human community. If the church is to be more than a mere political model, but also an agent for political change, this must be worked out in terms of a discussion of the church's proper calling.

The church of Jesus Christ must be understood in terms of past, present, and future. It is a token of the past because in its midst God has renewed the creative purposes which had become thwarted by sin. It is a sign of the future, because it manifests the first fruits of a Kingdom that is yet to come in its fulness. Its present calling cannot be understood apart from these past and future relations; in a world in which sin and sorrow characterize human activity, the church is called to be both a model and agent of healing. Of course, neither the Church nor our understanding of it is yet made perfect. In the present, we can only hope for a glimpse of God's original plan, and for "signs of the new order." Thus, the Apostle John rightly points to the necessary mixture of confidence and tentativeness that must characterize any discussion of the present condition of redeemed humanity: "Beloved, we are God's children now; it does not yet appear what we shall be" (I John 3:2).

[2]For an excellent discussion of this point, see Dillistone, *The Structure of Divine Society,* pp. 179-183.

# THE "MARKS OF THE TRUE CHURCH"

Although we cannot discuss all of the important ecclesiological questions in this present context, we will attempt to provide a framework for organizing our understanding of some crucial elements in the church's life and mission. In order to do this, we will take our point of departure from the description of the "marks of the true church" provided in the Belgic Confession of 1566. This Confession is accepted as a doctrinal standard by many Reformed churches, although what we will argue in this discussion should also be adaptable to some non-Reformed perspectives. On the question of the "marks of the true church," confessional documents in other traditions often mention only one or two of the three characteristics specified by the Belgic document: the Thirty-Nine Articles of the Anglican tradition, for example, lists only the first two—although there is no reason to think that Anglicans would be compelled to reject the third. Other ecclesiological traditions often focus on more formal or procedural features—such as the episcopacy; but even here we would not expect to find an outright rejection of the relevance of the features we will discuss.

The Belgic Confession puts the matter this way:

> The marks by which the true Church is known are these: If the pure doctrine of the gospel is preached therein; if she maintains the pure administration of the sacraments as instituted by Christ; if church discipline is exercised in punishing of sin (Art. 29).

In short, it stipulates that a properly formed worshiping community will be characterized by these three features: (1) the preaching of the word; (2) the observance of a sacramental life; and (3) the maintenance of standards of Christian discipline.

What the Reformation church had in mind when it stipulated these characteristics was at least this: that there ought to be formal occasions within the life of the institutional church when believers (1) listen to sermons, (2) observe sacraments, such as the Lord's supper, and (3) hold each other accountable, through some specified disciplinary process, for responsible Christian behavior.

What might have been the rationale for singling out these three aspects of church life? It is not difficult to think of one. First of all, the body of Christians must be a *listening* community, not a gathering of individuals met together for convenience or by human design. It is a community called into being by a word that comes from a nonhuman source, namely God. And it is a community called together continually to receive that word for correction, guidance, and edification. Secondly, it is a community that is *being served* by the God who calls it together. This is one important function of the sacrament of communion— to come to the Lord's table to be fed and served by the living Lord. Third, the Christian community is *in a process of growth,* of being shaped and disciplined in the life of discipleship.

This schema gives us a way of classifying different types of communities, secular as well as religious, in terms of an over-emphasis on one or another of these marks. A despotism would be a type of *listening* community, where the governing policies are the results of the commands of the despot, often arbitrary ones. The communes of the recent counter-culture often have a definitely *sacramental* style to them, although their shared communion, often based on a series of common emotional "highs," can quickly dissolve into anarchy. And there are communities which are based on a common commitment to a central *discipline,* or set of rules. The Boy Scouts come to mind as a kind of legalistic community of this sort. ·

In the Christian community there ought to be a profound unity to these three aspects of its life. The word that comes to it from beyond the borders of human experience is not an arbitrary word. It is the word of the servant-Lord who furthermore speaks to us and serves us for the purpose of building us up in the life of joyful obedience.

Thus far our comments have been meant as an explanation of the intentions of the writers of the Confession. But as a discussion of proper features of the church, in the broadest sense of "church," these stipulations are quite restricted. The Confession limits its commentary here, for the most part, to the "institutional" church—that body of persons which meets for worship and sacramental ceremony in a building at specified times, with appointed leaders, and so on. Furthermore, no reference is made to that body of persons *in action* in the world. We have here a reference only to the internal life of the institutional church.

Without pretending that in doing so we are any longer pursuing the actual intentions of the Confession's writers, we will propose that their formulation of the "marks of the true church" can be extended to two further dimensions of the life of the Christian community: its "internal" life beyond the confines of the institutional church, and its mission in the larger human community.

## THE SCOPE OF CHRISTIAN COMMUNITY

In suggesting that the church extends beyond its institutional setting, we are acknowledging a distinction that is often made between the church as "institute" and the church as "organism." As we will understand this distinction here the latter includes the former: thus we could portray the situation in terms of a little circle within a large circle. The smaller circle is made up of the matters already alluded to: the formal preaching of the word, sacramental ceremonies, official discipline—plus such matters as making budgets, electing or appointing officers, and the like. We will refer to these features as formal, ceremonial, and institutional, with the understanding that we are thereby singling out functions which are important and necessary to the life of the Christian community.

The larger circle, which symbolizes additional activities and functions that occur within the context of Christian community, includes at least two other kinds of phenomena: first, there are other Christian institutions and near-institutions. Consider the role of the Christian liberal arts college.

This kind of educational community is also a part of the community of the people of God; specifically, it is a gathering of individuals whose task it is to acknowledge the Lordship of Christ over educational and intellectual matters. It is itself a complex community which is part of a larger one: it has an institutional dimension, as well as many formal and informal activities and functions within its domain. The Christian family is also a kind of institutionalized grouping, as are various Bible study groups, youth organizations, and other special interest groups which function as a part of the church in the broad sense.

Second, there are many informal activities and groupings, such as bull sessions, parties, recreational events, and the like, which can also be thought of as manifestations of Christian community.

The relationship between the smaller circle, the institutional church, and the larger circle, the Christian community in its broadest scope, can be thought of in this way: the institutional church is the formal, ceremonial center of the life of the Christian community. Again, to use terms like "formal" and "ceremonial" is not to opt for mere "formalism" in Christian worship. We use these terms to point to a central function of the institutionalized worshiping community.

In the institutional church, Christians are in an important sense a *gathered* people. They are not only gathered from the variety of activities in which they participate in "the world." They are also gathered from various substantively Christian functions. The preaching of the word in the context of organized worship is not the only means by which Christians listen for God's revealed message. We often encounter his word in private or family devotions, in formal and informal discussions and bull sessions, through reading books and articles. Similarly, we often have fellowship with God in other than ceremonial sacramental settings—a fortunate thing for evangelical Christians, given their infrequent sacramental gatherings. And we are disciplined in other ways than through formal ecclesiastical channels; for example, through Christian counseling and in friendly arguments with other Christians.

Why, then, these institutional offices and functions at all? This is, of course, a question that has been seriously posed by many Christians in recent years, with the result that for some people other institutions and groupings within the larger Christian community have taken over the functions of the institutional church. For example, the house church has often tended to absorb the marks of the institutional church into a kind of family unit.

It may be that we are being called in this age to experiment with new forms and structures for the institutional aspect of the Christian community. But there are important reasons for preserving the practice of gathering as Christians from diverse subgroups for the purpose of ceremonial worship. First, it may be that as human beings we have deep ceremonial and ritualistic needs that will be met, whether we consciously recognize them or not. For all of its conscious attempts at informality and anti-institutionalism, the radical student movement of the 1960s developed a strong ceremonial structure. It came to recognize charismatic leaders who were expected to inspire crowds gathered for protest; it had litanies ("What do we want?" "Peace!" "When do we want it?" "Now!"), chants ("All we are saying is give peace a chance"), hymns ("We shall overcome"), rites of initiation and sacraments (at the 1969 "March on Washington" I was struck by the number of people passing food and drink around; some were even distributing sandwiches and brownies that they had prepared for the purpose of sharing); and it had a dress code and other forms of "discipline."

Second, ceremony provides us with a means of making commitments. The marriage ceremony plays an important role in this respect. It is a way of ceremonially acting out one's intention to be a faithful partner in a public sealing of a relationship. Similarly, by adopting with other Christians a common ceremonial posture of submission to the word, of gathering around a common table, or pledging obedience to a shared discipline, we are publicly sealing our commitment to be the community that God calls us to be.

But, thirdly, there seems to be a more profound sense in which ceremonial gatherings can be a means of actualizing our reality as the community of the people of God. Gerhard von Rad points to this dimension in Israel's understanding of its festivals.

> It was only the community assembled for a festival that by recitation and ritual brought Israel in the full sense of the word into being: in her own person she really and truly entered into the historic situation to which the festival in question was related. When Israel ate the Passover, clad as for a journey, staff in hand, sandals on her feet, and in the haste of departure (Ex. xii, 11), she was manifestly doing more than merely remembering the Exodus; she was entering into the saving event of the Exodus itself, and participating in it in a quite "actual" way.[3]

Similarly, Christian worship is a way of identifying with the past events of the Christian community. But it is also an eschatological sign of the Kingdom that is yet to come in its fulness. By ceremonially submitting to a common word, sacrament, and discipline, we are posturing as the unified people of God. But, of course, we are *not* yet that in the fullest sense. Indeed the church is often a motley and diverse crowd. But by that common ceremonial involvement we are pointing to the day when what we now experience ceremonially will be a realized fact. In this sense, the life of the institutional church has a value similar to that which is often claimed for simulation games: for a white suburbanite to "play out" the role of a ghetto black is to take that identity on himself and to take a step toward a sense of unity with the ghetto situation.

In all of this we should not be taken as suggesting that the life of the institutional church is *merely* ceremonial. God actually speaks to us in the formal proclamation of the word; he actually serves us in the sacramental celebration;

[3]*Old Testament Theology* (New York: Harper, 1965), II, 164.

and our lives can actually improve within the framework of church discipline. But these formal institutional functions are also a means by which the formalized events become a part of, "spill over" into, the informal, nonecclesiastical patterns of the Christian community, so that in all aspects of our individual and communal lives we may become a listening people who are served and disciplined by the living Lord. As James Gustafson puts it:

> Throughout a social interpretation of the Church runs a double theme. The Church is marked by an inwardness, a common quality of life and commitment to certain truths. It is marked by an outwardness, signs and symbols, books and rites, by which persons of general cultural knowledge can designate it. It is both external and internal; it is outwardly institutional and inwardly communal. The double character of its life is necessary; the most intimate sense of unity depends upon the outward expressions given to the past life and events remembered in the community.[4]

## CHURCH AND KINGDOM

We have been using two senses of the term church, a narrower and a broader sense. However, in some ecclesiological discussions different sets of distinctions are employed: most common are the distinctions between visible and invisible church, and between church and kingdom.

Our present discussion can be related to these distinctions as follows. The visible church can be thought of as including all manifestations of Christian obedience and service which are presently observable, including both institutional and noninstitutional phenomena. The invisible church, then, would include at least two kinds of phenomena: all such manifestations of the rule of Christ which have occurred in the past and which will occur in the future, but which are not contemporary phenomena and all of those bonds and

[4]*Treasure in Earthen Vessels* (New York: Harper, 1961), pp. 12f.

**63**

relationships which presently exist, but which are not visible to human perception—for example, the mutual concerns which unite Christians secretly worshiping under totalitarian governments with North American Christians.

When thinking of church in contrast to kingdom, we do well to consider the church as denoting all past, present, and future manifestations of the *institutional* church, with the kingdom comprised of all else that falls under the rule of Christ, but also *including* the institutional church. The institutional church, then, is one among many manifestations of the kingdom of God, namely, that manifestation in which the people of God are gathered for ceremonial worship and related activities.

The distinction between church and kingdom, as thus explained, is exactly similar to our distinction between the narrow and broad senses of church. The church, narrowly conceived, is the kingdom institutionalized for specific purposes. Similarly, a Christian liberal arts college is the kingdom being manifested in the pursuit of *academic* obedience to the rule of Christ; the Christian family is the kingdom manifested in distinctively *familial* actvities; a Christian softball team is the kingdom manifested in attempts at *recreational* obedience to the rule of Christ.

The last of these examples may appear facetious. Since it is not so intended, some explanation might be appropriate. Christians are called to show forth the rule of Christ in all spheres of human activity, including the area of recreational pursuits. For this reason there is nothing wrong in principle with forming an organization like the Fellowship of Christian Athletes. Indeed, properly conceived, such a group might perform an important service on behalf of the Christian community. To profess Christ as Lord over all of life should have important implications for our understanding of the appropriate forms that competition might take, the relationship between participating in games and receiving monetary rewards for that participation, the possibility for humanizing patterns of interaction between athletic antagonists, players and coaches, teams and owners, and so on.

Christians who are professional athletes (that concept could also do with some careful Christian analysis) ought to be concerned about such matters; at the very least they ought to ask what it means for the psychological, economic, and cultural patterns of their activity to proclaim that Christ is Lord over their athletic pursuits. The thought that there might be an organized context in which Christians struggle together with these questions points to a much-needed area for Christian communal dialogue.

The problem is that often such organizations take the commonly accepted answers to questions about competition, the "business" of athletics, and so on, for granted. Thus, they limit their concern to questions like: How can I maintain a high degree of spirituality as a football player? How can I use my mode of employment as a means of "leading others to Christ?"

The same objections can be raised with respect to Christian businessmen's groups. It is typical of such fellowships that they purposely seem to ignore questions about what the Lordship of Christ means for economic practices. Instead of asking, "What does it mean to proclaim Christ's rule in the writing of an insurance policy?" they tend to ask, "How can I, as a successful insurance salesman, *also* engage in personal evangelism?" thus ignoring questions about the relationship between Christian commitment and economic activity as such.

Because of urgent needs in these and other areas, it is important to stress the necessity for forming Christian sub-groups who gather for discussion and dialogue at some point midway between the institutional church and individual vocational pursuits. The Christian community has often been presented with a false choice on questions concerning corporate witness. We have often assumed that the Christian address to social issues must either take the form of official pronouncements on the part of the institutional church (political sermons, ecclesiastical decrees) or that such matters must be pursued on an individual basis. A third alternative is for Christians to form groups which are not ecclesiastically sponsored but which serve as a basis for collective witness in various spheres of activities.

Consider yet another concrete proposal. In various political decision-making bodies, at urban, state, and national levels, there are Christian officeholders. They are likely to be, in any given situation, a diverse lot, representing different ecclesiastical loyalties and a variety of political identifications. Presently, such persons often do gather on a regular basis for "spiritual" fellowship. Why could this means of association not be taken a step further? Why could they not reason as follows: "We are persons of various theological stripes and political persuasions, but we have one thing in common: each of us confesses that Jesus Christ is his or her Lord. Let's discuss what this means for the actual legislative decisions we must make this week. We won't require unanimity of ideology or political commitment; but we will hold each other responsible for answering these questions: As I vote on specific matters of legislation this week, how do I see myself as being motivated by a desire to acknowledge Jesus Christ as *king*? What, if any, specifically Christian concerns bear on the decisions I face? For a while, let's just each try to articulate answers to those questions and not argue about our respective answers. Maybe later on we may agree to begin discussing the main patterns of agreement and disagreement that emerge from our regular discussions. But at the very least we *owe* each other an account of the Christian basis for our political pursuits."

Is it unrealistic to expect a common Christian commitment to this minimal kind of mutual accountability and correction? If it is, then is it also unrealistic to desire such a commitment? If Christian politicians cannot agree on the program outlined above, we can outline an even simpler program: they can meet to discuss why it is impossible and/ or undesirable for them to continue meeting!

In every area of activity and association Christian attitudes and relationships must be characterized by something like the three marks of the true church. Whether they are gathered for the purpose of seeking guidance in politics, academic pursuits, athletic activities, familial relations, Christians must adopt the posture of a *listening* people who have received a word for guidance in all areas of life; they must acknowledge the presence of a *servant*-Lord whose redemptive work extends to human brokenness and sin wherever their influence is felt; and they must seek to be *disciplined* by the word of the servant-Lord in every word and deed.

## THE "EXTERNAL" MISSION

We have discussed the life of both the institutional church and the larger Christian community. We must now ask how this community is to relate to the even larger human community of which it is a part.

The marks of the true church also have analogies to important elements in the external mission of the Christian community in the world. First, while the people of God, viewed from the perspective of their internal life, must form a listening community, they must also function as a proclaiming people in the larger society. The message they have received is not to be hidden from the world. The people who have heard the good news must also bear the message to others. Second, the people who have been served by Jesus Christ must in turn become servants in the world he came to save. Third, as those who have been—or are in the process of being—disciplined by God's word, they must become discipliners in the world. These three requirements, which we have drawn as analogies to the institutional functions of preaching, sacraments, and discipline, correspond closely to the biblical "offices" of prophet, priest, and king.

To see these as aspects of the church's mission in the world provides us with a helpful way of sorting out the diverse missiological emphases that we actually observe among Christian groups. There are those who view the church's mission largely in proclamatory terms. From their perspective Christians are called primarily to a verbal articulation of the gospel. This is certainly true of those who place great emphasis on personal witnessing and mass evangelism—activities they often understand purely in terms of "getting the message out." But this tendency can also be observed among many who view the gospel in more social terms, for whom Christian witness seems on occasion to be something best carried out by signing newspaper advertisements and carrying placards.

On the other hand, there are Christians who see the primary calling of the church as manifested in "servant" activities. In contrast to the "proclaimers" these Christians often devalue verbal presentations as mere talk. That brand of missiology which stresses "incarnational" themes is closely aligned with this servant category. Great emphasis is placed on the intrinsic value of Christian presence among a certain subgroup of human beings, for the purpose of "casting our lot with them"—and with very little emphasis on the need for getting a message, beyond that of one's actions, across.

Finally, there are Christians who insist on the need for imposing "disciplinary" patterns on the larger society. In this group there are those who attempt to promote legislative changes in order to bring society into closer conformity to Christian patterns of behavior. Here we often find strong formal agreement among Christians who have very different, even conflicting, legislative visions. Some want all citizens, whether Christians or non-Christians, to conform to specific patterns of Sunday-observance, sexual behavior, and alcohol use (or non-use); others are more concerned with civil rights legislation, environment policies, and the like, as proper objects of Christian legislative concern.

It may be that no individual or group perfectly exemplifies any of these approaches in unmixed form. These are, however, discernible tendencies among different Christian groups.

Properly understood, each of these emphases is in fact an important aspect of the church's mission in the world. In an important sense, they complement each other in a well-formed mission. Without pretending to develop a complete theology of missions or evangelism here, let us briefly consider the significance of each of these elements, with special application to the *political* mission of the church.

First, we are called as a redeemed people to proclaim God's word in the world. This is an emphasis dear to the hearts of those Christians who call themselves evangelicals, and rightly so, for Christianity is rooted in the evangel, the good *news*. Our Christian faith is a response to our having "*heard* the joyful sound." Christianity is a religion of words, of information. It is not merely words, but it is at least words. The God of the Scriptures is a speaking God—not *just* a speaking God, but at least a speaking God. However we may understand the theological construction of a "propositional revelation," there is no way of avoiding this: Christians have received a *message* from God, one they are in turn compelled to proclaim in the world.

God has spoken to human beings. As a consequence his people cannot help being a speaking, proclaiming people. We may often speak too much or misleadingly, but that does not mean that we are wrong in thinking that we are called to speak on God's behalf. Furthermore, God has addressed himself to the totality of human existence and experience. He has spoken a word which has application to politics, among other things. And so we must speak about politics; we must attempt to articulate a faithful message for the political realm.

This message, however, must be one that is *for* the political realm. This points to the importance of the second aspect, the "priestly" identification with the world to which we are called to relate as servants. In the Old Testament, the prophet represented God before the people. The priest on the other hand represented the people before God; he brought their concerns, their offerings and prayers, into the divine presence. The Christian mission must combine these two functions. We bring a message to a world whose needs and concerns we can faithfully represent before God. We must, in some important sense, identify with the political needs and sufferings of the world.

At the very least the call to servanthood requires us to be able to communicate about and within actual political processes. To draw an extreme analogy, missionaries would not be faithfully fulfilling the mandate to proclaim God's word to a pagan society if they presented their message in a language or concepts not understandable by that society. As a minimal requirement they must identify with the linguistic and conceptual patterns of the people they preach to. Similarly, we must have some kind of grasp of the actual processes, concepts, and problems of politics if we are going to articulate God's will for that sphere of activity.

But verbal articulation and specific acts of servanthood are not enough. We must also seek to alter the structures of the larger human community. It would be naive to state this requirement without acknowledging the important arguments of those Christians who insist that while Christians ought to be very sensitive to the unjust patterns of society, they ought *not* directly to attempt to alter those patterns but should confront sinful structures by being an alternative community, by proclaiming God's judgment on corporate injustice, and by suffering with those who experience the oppression of that injustice. We will consider this perspective at length in the next chapter. Suffice it here to say that we shall dissent from this refusal to engage in attempts at political change.

Our threefold emphasis here is the political application of a case that applies to all evangelistic activity. The Christian gospel is not to be proclaimed as a blanket impersonal message; it is a word *to* human individuals and it meets them in their wholeness and uniqueness. The verbal articulation of the gospel then cannot be divorced from genuine efforts to empathize with the actual needs of specific unbelievers. Nor can it be divorced from a concern to see their lives fulfilled under the healing discipline of Christ's rule.

## IDENTIFYING WITH OPPRESSION

In recent years it has become common in some Christian quarters to describe the Christian calling in terms of "identifying with the oppressed." This is an important emphasis. As we will see a little further on, it points to something at the very heart of the Bible's central and special concern with the plight of the economically deprived. Before discussing that issue, however, we must critically examine the general theme of identifying with the oppressed.

To get clear about the way in which Christians are called to identify with the oppressed, it is necessary to ask two significant questions. First, what is the nature of the oppression that is an important object of biblical concern? It is difficult to avoid the impression that this term is often used to refer to somewhat diverse situations when it is employed in the current dialogue: women are oppressed by a male-dominated system which is perpetuated through sexist stereotypes and role-models. Third World peoples are oppressed by the rich and powerful nations. Homosexua experience oppression in the armed forces. The elderly are victimized by oppressive "age-ist" attitudes.

It is not always easy to discern the basis for kinship among these groups. A homosexual officer in the United States Air Force may indeed suffer because of his sexual preferences, but much of his suffering is due to his having chosen an occupational environment in which sexual orientation is a matter of official concern. There does not seem to be an analogous element of choice in the plight of Chilean peasants. Similarly, a white teen-age girl in a Toronto suburb, whatever the discrimination she may face in her lifetime, will have many more opportunities to decide her economic destiny than will her counterpart on an Alberta Indian reservation.

My point is not to argue that it is wrong to call each of these groups oppressed, but to show that supporters of a variety of liberation movements seem willing to operate with a rather fluid notion of oppression—which makes it all the more difficult to understand why they often draw the lines where they do. Many feminists, for example, are willing to admit that sexist males are also "oppressed," in that they too suffer from the need to conform to stereotypes—in this case to the expectation that a male will be "strong" and "rational." Why not extend the concept further to include all economic and political power-brokers who are driven by a compulsion to manipulate and coerce?

Indeed, there seem to be important parallels between the situation of many of the powerful today and that of Zacchaeus, as he is portrayed in the Gospel. By our contemporary "radical" standards, Zacchaeus was a member of the rich and powerful class. Yet in spite of popular resentment toward the unjust and manipulative practices of the tax-collectors Jesus had compassion on him. The first half of the common contemporary complaint against Jesus—that he associated with *"tax-collectors* and sinners" (see Luke 15:1-2 and Matt. 9:11)—is seldom mentioned by Christians today who cite Jesus' association with the outcasts of society in support of their calls for "liberation."

The oppression the Bible demands we confront appears in many forms. It certainly includes political and economic oppression, and we have no excuse for dismissing the emphasis of those who would call that to our attention. But the oppression caused by sin is also more than this: teen-age drug users in Middle America, millionaires struggling against alcoholism, used car salesmen experiencing the process of painful divorce proceedings—all of these suffer from oppression, and are thereby candidates for a ministry of Christian compassion.

The second question is: How shall we identify with the needs of the oppressed? The appropriate Christian response to oppression must be at least as complex as that oppression itself; one can recommend a simple formula for the work of liberating the oppressed only if one has a simple notion of oppression.

Here too the case of Zacchaeus helps provide us with guidelines. To liberate power-brokers and male sexists from their oppression requires a change of attitude on their part; this would be admitted on all sides. But can we say less in our designs for the liberation of the economically and politically oppressed? A change in the economic structures of Chile will not automatically usher in the kingdom of God

for peasants anymore than the elimination of sexist stereotypes will do so for middle-class American women.

Unless human beings are willing to forsake the futile patterns of pretending to be their own lords, they will be
liberated from one form of oppression only to be victimized
by other forms. Political and economic restructurings are
important elements in the total kingdom picture, but they
are not by themselves the total picture.

With the complexities of oppression in mind, how shall
we identify with the oppressed? It should be clear that each
Christian cannot identify with oppression in all of its forms.
When we say that the church must deal with oppression in
all of its manifestations, we mean to insist that the total
ministry of the church, taken in its entirety, must include a
concern with a diversity of matters. Each Christian must
support the total ministry of the church; but that does not
mean that each will do so in exactly the same manner.

Nor is it clear that each instance of oppression will be
identified with in exactly the same way. There was probably
a significant sense in which Hitler was oppressed by his own
mad lust for power. In what way should a Christian have
identified with Hitler? There might have been a point in
Hitler's career when some Christian could have sincerely
attempted to understand Hitler's fears and compulsions in
order to bring words of Christian hope and healing to him
as a unique individual. Indeed, it is not impossible, even
now, to reflect on Hitler's personal situation in such a way
that one can in some sense "empathize" with a life in which
compulsive hatred leads a person to such vile courses of
action. From one perspective, Hitler's case is sad and piti-
ful. But in his case it is impossible *merely* to focus on these
matters without also being aware of the inestimable pain
and destruction which were caused by his patterns of behavior. It is very unlikely that any Christian, in such a
situation, could conscientiously permit himself to ignore the
facts of the larger context in order to identify with Hitler's
personal oppression.

On the other hand, there are many situations in which

**73**

Christians *are* required to identify with felt needs and fears in a perfectly straightforward way. Christians must reach out in compassion to the aged, the physically suffering, starving children, and so on. We must in a very important sense share in their agonies. And this must be done, not out of a masochistic desire to punish ourselves, but as our mode of participation in the redemptive ministry of Jesus Christ. This ministry, as we have already stressed, must include our conveying a message of love and healing, our serving the actual needs of those who are oppressed, and our attempts to manifest the disciplining rule of Christ in those broken situations.

## SERVING THE POOR

There is a very central place among the concerns of the biblical message for the economically deprived. The Bible's special emphasis on this class of human beings is so unambiguous that it is fair to say that a concern for the poor is a fundamental test of the faithfulness of the Christian community. John Calvin is not guilty of overstatement when he insists that

> God sends us the poor as his receivers. And although the alms are given to mortal creatures, yet God accepts and approves them and puts them to one's account, as if we had placed in his hands that which we give to the poor.[5]

This emphasis is pervasive in the Old Testament. Consider one example. In Joshua's last speech to Israel he represents the Lord as reminding Israel that it is presently benefiting from the labors of the previous occupants of their land: "I gave you a land on which you had not labored, and cities which you had not built, and you dwell therein; you eat the fruit of vineyards and oliveyards which you did not plant" (Josh. 24:13). Later in Israel's history, the

[5]Sermon on Deut. 15:11-15, quoted by W. Fred Graham, in *The Constructive Revolutionary: John Calvin and his Socio-Economic Impact* (Richmond: John Knox, 1971), p. 69.

prophet Amos also refers to these same possessions, but with a very different message: "You have built houses of hewn stone, but you shall not dwell in them; you have planted vineyards, but you shall not drink their wine" (Amos 5:11). At one time, the Lord had given Israel houses others had built and vineyards others had planted; now he is going to take the houses and vineyards *Israel* had produced and give them away.

Why the reversal? Amos's answer is plain: "Because you trample upon the poor and take from him exactions of wheat . . . and you turn aside the needy in the gate" (Amos 5:11-12). Israel had received its possessions by God's grace; but their gracious Lord is not oblivious to how his people use and distribute his gifts. Their concern for the needy is a test of their faithfulness to his will.

The mandate to be concerned about the plight of the poor does not disappear in the New Testament, as is obvious in Mary's song concerning the redemptive mission of her son (see Luke 1:52), Jesus' "least of these" discourse (Matt. 25:31-46), and the condemnation of Babylon in the last book of the Bible, because "the merchants of the earth have grown rich with the wealth of her wantonness" (Rev. 18:3). To be sure, the frequent references to the poor in the Epistles deal mainly with disadvantaged *Christians* (as examples see James 2 and I Timothy 5:16), which is also characteristic of John Calvin's comments on the subject; but as C. E. B. Cranfield perceptively remarks:

> whereas in Paul's (and Calvin's) days a large proportion of the Christian community must have been very poor, at the present time Christians of the west share the affluence of their nations to a great extent, and in the poorer countries the Christians will often be among the less poor members of the community. In view of the different circumstances of the Church, we ought surely to put less emphasis today on the special claim of the saints, and more on the claims of human distress generally.[6]

[6]*A Commentary on Romans 12-13* (Scottish Journal of Theology Occasional Papers, No. 12; Edinburgh: Oliver and Boyd, 1965), p. 48.

The church must identify in a special way with the needs of the poor. But how should it do so? This question is an important tactical one which must be touched on here in the hope of achieving further clarity in a matter that has a crucial bearing on the church's mission. Let us make some brief observations.

First, a recognition of the centrality of the mandate to minister to the poor does not automatically rule out some form of ministry to the rich and the powerful. This can be seen by considering the implications of two conflicting theories in their starkest versions. On one view, all individuals are victimized by the formative power of "systemic" economic and political attitudes, which each individual has come to "internalize." The self-images and economic/cultural attitudes of the rich and the poor, then, are on the whole determined by their social and economic status—thus the concept of "class consciousness." Were we to adopt this perspective, it would seem that an economically powerful person is not only a proper candidate for Christian compassion, but we may well *serve* the cause of the poor by attempting to sensitize him to his own victimization. On the other view, the rich exploit the poor by their own conscious and deliberate choices. If this account is correct, it may be a service to the poor to attempt to convince the rich that they ought to make *different* choices.

On either view, then—and, it would seem, for any mediating perspective—an initial attempt to befriend the rich and to make any legitimate identification with their needs that we can ("meeting them where they are") might be a legitimate tactic with respect to bettering the lot of the poor. There can be no doubt that this possibility presents Christians with many temptations to rationalize illegitimate activity. But this is to say that Christians are often faced with *difficult* decisions. Jesus himself launched a difficult project when he sought out Zacchaeus, but it may be that we are called to follow his example by saying to the rich and the powerful, "I must stay at your house today" (Luke 19:5).

Second, the question of how our personal possessions

are to be utilized in the service of the poor also has to be considered in the light of difficult tactical decisions. For one thing we must be careful not to base an entire theology of wealth on such biblical passages as the one reporting Christ's encounter with the rich young ruler (Luke 18:18-30). It may be that Christ's purpose here was to insist, as he did in other cases, that a person must be *willing* to give up whatever counts as his or her dearest earthly loyalty for the sake of discipleship. Jesus apparently did not make the same demand of Joseph of Arimathea, unless he exempted such possessions as tombs and clean linen; and it is not obvious that the approved arrangement with Zacchaeus—whereby half of his goods were given to the poor, plus a repayment of fourfold the amount of everything that had been gained by fraud—depleted the tax collector's savings.

But the advice to the young ruler is not completely irrelevant to our own economic decision-making, so that it is important that we attempt to understand that advice properly as it applies to our situation. In one sense each Christian should treat his or her possessions as belonging to Jesus Christ to be used in the service of the oppressed as our Lord directs us to do so. If this means literally giving all to the economically deprived, we must decide whether this should be done in a single act or by an extended process of giving. We must also decide whether we can legitimately count that which goes into the support of our own vocation as a way of giving to the poor. An important question at this point is whether one ought to give all to the poor in such a way as also to become totally dependent on the charity of others. These are not meant as light-hearted questions, but as indications of the kinds of considerations that must go into a careful and perhaps complicated theological perspective on personal possessions.

## THE CONCERN FOR JUSTICE

The biblical call to identify with the oppressed, especially with the economically oppressed, is directly related

77

to its mandate to promote a society characterized by justice. Here we must examine some dimensions of our requirement that the mission of the church include "kingly" disciplining activity.

The church must attempt to bring society into conformity to Christian standards for human interaction. In saying this, however, we are not endorsing all the attempts that have actually been made along these lines. Indeed, many of these attempts are wrongheaded precisely on the grounds that they have failed to recognize the central biblical plea for justice.

Consider the matter of sexual behavior. The Bible condemns sexual promiscuity and adultery on the grounds that sexual intimacy cannot be properly experienced apart from covenantal faithfulness. Only in that context can sexual intercourse serve to express mutual commitment and a profound knowing of one another. Within the community bound together by an explicit covenant of faithfulness between God and human beings, and between Christian persons themselves, departures from a commitment to the norm of marital fidelity must be considered as serious breaches of faith.

But what ought to be the Christian posture toward those who do *not* acknowledge biblical covenantal norms? More specifically, in what ways ought Christians attempt to influence the sexual attitudes of those who are not Christians? At the very least, Christians ought to regret the existence of indications of widespread sexual promiscuity— not because they have "hang-ups" about sex, but because of a legitimate conviction that sexual patterns have important connections to other serious dimensions of human existence. The inability to pledge sexual fidelity is an indication of a problem with fidelity as such. The self-images and compulsions involved in promiscuous pursuits do not function in isolation from the rest of human life.

But Christians must not merely regret these patterns; they must attempt to provide an antidote, through the proclamation of a better way. In scholarship, preaching, and evangelistic activity we must expose the assumptions and implications of sexual anarchy as a part of our proclamation of a message that is, among other things, good news for those suffering from the varieties of sexual oppression.

We should not, however, attempt to promote legislation whose primary *purpose* is to force non-Christians to conform to specifically Christian patterns of sexual behavior. This may seem on the face of it like a denial of the proposal that Christians ought to bring society into conformity to Christian standards of human interaction. But we must not forget that on Christian standards people must freely offer their lives in service to God and neighbor. Laws designed simply to force human beings into grudging conformity will not promote this goal.

There are a host of problems that can be legitimately raised in this area. As we struggle with them there are two assumptions that ought to be kept clearly in mind. First, Christians ought to regret widespread patterns of sexual promiscuity. But, second, Christians ought not to act in such a way that the sole purpose of their action is to prohibit non-Christians from behaving in a promiscuous manner. No Christian ought to promote "blue laws" simply because he or she is upset by the thought that someone somewhere may be watching a pornographic movie.

A concern to promote justice must be based on a desire that human beings be free to pursue the interests and projects that flow from their fundamental life commitments, *however regrettable those choices may be from a Christian point of view*. Not that restrictions on such pursuits are never called for: opportunities for sexual promiscuity must be restricted when it infringes seriously on the genuine rights of others—for example, on the rights of children. But the Christian's "right" to rest in the knowledge that no one is enjoying pornography is *not* one such genuine right.

This pattern of respect for the choices of others is exhibited by God himself. When Adam and Eve chose to rebel against his will, God did not destroy them on that account; nor did he attempt to exact their *grudging* obedience. Having made their choice, they were free to pursue its implications. Of course, God could legitimately point out the cursedness of the situation they had chosen. He could even bar them from the Garden because they had rejected the requirements for inhabiting it. Ultimately, sinful persons must face up to the real possibility that the utter loneliness and alienation of hell is the logical outcome of their rebellious project. But none of this needs to be viewed as vindictive manipulation on God's part. On the contrary, these matters are the result of his fundamental respect for the actual choices his creatures pursue. It is a terrible matter when Christians attempt to exercise a pattern of coercive lordship which God himself has refused.

Our attempts to engage in a kingly disciplining of society, then, must not be *motivated* by a desire to coerce or manipulate others. There is no value in restricting behavior *just* because it is sinful behavior. We are justified in promoting legislation only when it is aimed at a more equitable distribution of rights and opportunities.

It is in this light that we must view our obligation to promote political change for the sake of the poor and oppressed. If the greed and covetousness of a rich man were being manifested in such a way that no one but him was being oppressed by his activities, we would not have the right to attempt to change his behavior by coercion. We should preach to him, even plead with him to forsake his self-destructive ways, but we ought not try to "legislate" his behavior. Naturally, oppressive economic activity does not occur in a vacuum. The wickedness of the rich and powerful regularly manifests itself in the form of sins against the poor and oppressed. When such is the case, Christians must renounce any personal rights to pursue riches and power for selfish gain, in order to plead and lobby on behalf of the deprived and afflicted.

## A COMPLEX MISSION

The total mission of the people of God in the world

is a very complex one. Viewed internally, the church must engage in an extended effort to *be* a certain kind of community. It must listen to God's Word, experience the healing provided by the servant-Lord, and grow in grace and knowledge. But it must also be an active presence in the larger community, proclaiming the word it has received, responding to the actual needs and suffering it finds, and attempting to promote patterns and practices which approximate God's standards of justice and righteousness. Neither its internal life nor its external mission can be neglected. It cannot be a force for justice in the world unless it is also itself a community that has been shaped by the justice and mercy of God. But it cannot be the community God calls it to be unless it is also the agent of God's redemptive mission in the world.

The task of faithfully responding to the church's complex mandate is of necessity a difficult one, involving many profound decisions and struggles. For this reason it is necessary to maintain a high level of mutual accountability and a spirit of solidarity among individuals who are pursuing the diverse functions which are all parts of the church's mission.

Furthermore, it must be acknowledged by all parties that there are no simple formulas to provide the church with easy solutions in its complex decision-making. The commandments and directives given for the church's guidance, whether they are "handed down" from Mount Sinai, Geneva, Garden Grove, or 475 Riverside Drive, will serve to build up the life and mission of the church only if they are subject to careful and prayerful interpretation and scrutiny. In the Old Testament God did not provide Israel with a set of disconnected arbitrary commands, nor with a checklist of "essentials for church growth," but with a vision of what a community could be if it lived in obedience to the true God. Knowing the difficulty of appropriating that vision to the rough places in the wilderness, Israel's God went beyond issuing official pronouncements; he also promised his personal presence in the midst of their struggles and

81

deliberations: "Behold, I send an angel before you, to guard you on the way and to bring you to the place which I have prepared. Give heed to him and hearken to his voice . . . for my name is in him" (Exodus 23:20-21).

The same promise is extended to the New Testament church. When Jesus gave his disciples instructions to prepare them for when he would ascend to the Father, he also went beyond the stipulation that they must keep his commandments, adding: "And I will pray the Father, and he will give you another Counselor, to be with you forever, even the Spirit of truth . . . and [he] will be in you" (John 14:15-17).

*Emmanuel.* "I will be God to you." The personal presence of God is a crucial factor at every point of the discussion in political theology. It is because we have experienced the complex work of redemption in a personal way that we can commit ourselves to what often appears as a hopelessly complicated mission. In an older translation of the Heidelberg Catechism, Question 52 asks, "What comfort is it to thee that Christ *shall come again to judge the quick and the dead?*" The answer reads in part: "That in all my sorrows and persecutions, with uplifted head, I look for the self-same One who has before offered himself for me to the judgment of God, and removed from me all curse, to come again as Judge from heaven."

There are those who tremble and quake at the thought of divine judgment, but Christians do not need to do so; for we know that the one who will someday stand as our judge is "the self-same One" who has suffered in all ways that we have suffered, and whose love for us carried him to the cross.

The call to engage in the church's complex mission can also be met with this kind of comfort. The one who issues this call is himself a complex Lord. He has approached us as the proclaimer of a word, a servant-Lord, and a King who brings disciplined healing to our brokenness. But our experience is of a God who is "the self-same One" throughout all of these things. It is because of this experience of a

God whose redemptive mission to us is a complex unity that our required response—which might at first glance seem to be a matter that will be plagued with confusion and fragmentation—can be instead the occasion for an ever-expanding awareness of the riches of his grace.

# CHAPTER FIVE

# CONFRONTING THE "POWERS"

We must now take a clearer look at some questions related to our prescriptions concerning the "kingly" task of the Christian community. Is it permissible for Christians to attempt to gain political power? Is it proper to pursue justice within the present structures of political decision-making? Must we refuse to participate in any sphere of activity which requires the use of "coercion?"

These questions point, as we will see, to a controversial area of discussion among many contemporary Christians. To gain a proper focus on the issues at stake, we shall first note some recent studies of the Pauline references to "principalities and powers." Then we will examine some issues which bear specifically on the propriety of Christian involvement in the present political order.

## "PRINCIPALITIES AND POWERS"

Over the past two decades an important body of literature has come into being which deals with Pauline attitudes toward the civil order, especially with respect to the Apostle's frequent references to "principalities," "powers," and the like.[1] The following three passages are typical of these references in Paul.

> For I am sure that neither death, nor life, nor angels, nor principalities, nor things present, nor things to come, nor powers, nor height, nor depth, nor anything else in all creation, will be able to separate us from the love of, God in Christ Jesus our Lord (Rom. 8:38-39).

> For we do not have to wrestle against flesh and blood, but against principalities and powers, against the world rulers of this darkness, against the evil spirits in heavenly places (Eph. 6:12).

> For in him are all things created, which are in heaven and on earth, the visible and the invisible, whether thrones, dominions, principalities, powers; all things are created through him and for him (Col. 1:16).

We will not deal here with all of the details of current expositions of Paul's thought on this subject, but we must touch on some of the major points on which a consensus has emerged as well as on a few matters of disagreement.

It is now an accepted view that in at least some of the passages like those quoted, Paul is indicating his belief that a plurality of created "spiritual" powers or forces exists. These forces in some sense "stand behind" and "influence" the political life (in addition to other areas of human soci-

[1]The following is a selection of some important works that have appeared in English, listed chronologically: Hendrikus Berkhof, *Christ and the Powers* (Scottsdale, Pa.: Herald Press, 1962; originally published in Dutch in 1953); G. B. Caird, *Principalities and Powers: A Study in Pauline Theology* (Oxford: The Clarendon Press, 1956; the 1954 Chancellor's Lectures at Queen's University, Ontario); Oscar Cullmann, *The State in the New Testament* (New York: Scribners, 1956); Clinton Morrison, *The Powers That Be: Earthly Rulers and Demonic Powers in Romans 13:1-7* (Naperville, Ill.: Alec R. Allenson, 1960); Cyril H. Powell, *The Biblical Concept of Power* (London: Epworth Press, 1963); C. E. B. Cranfield, *A Commentary on Romans 12:13*; Albert H. van den Heuvel, *Those Rebellious Powers* (London: SCM Press, 1966); John Howard Yoder, *The Politics of Jesus*.

ety). Most scholars concede that this Pauline belief continues a line of development in biblical thought that seems already to begin early in the Old Testament, with references to a plurality of "gods" who are regularly described as rivaling in vain the power and authority of Israel's God. In Canaanite religions these gods were often closely associated with specific natural forces, such as fertility. Their status and functions later came to be ascribed (roughly) to angelic "ministers," "holy ones" (Ps. 89:6-8), and divine "messengers." These, in turn, later emerge—especially in the post-exilic period—as "folk angels" and "guardian angels" with specific national assignments (see Dan. 12:1).[2]

But if Paul's conception stands in this developing tradition, there are two qualifications we must make. First, Paul's views were worked out in the context of an interaction between this Old Testament legacy and what C. D. Morrison labels as a "Graeco-Roman concept of the State," which was commonly accepted by both pagans and Christians in Paul's time.[3] According to Morrison, Paul accepted the broad "cosmological" outlines of the Graeco-Roman perspective, but he rejected much of the specifically pagan religious content: for example, he reinterpreted the pagan conception of *daimones* in the light of the Old Testament's angelological tradition.[4] Thus, as Cyril Powell observes, Paul's views can be found "at the point where Jewish ideas concerning 'angels' and Hellenistic ideas concerning astral and cosmic powers intersect."[5]

Second, it also seems to be generally agreed that Paul went a step beyond the Old Testament tradition by at least partially "depersonalizing" the Powers. Hendrikus Berkhof sees two emphases in Old Testament angelology: angels are *personal* beings, and they *influence* human affairs. Paul did not cling to the first of these factors; thus, "we must set

[2]For further comments on this line of biblical development, cf. Powell, *op. cit.*, p. 16, and Caird, *op. cit.*, pp. 1-15.
[3]Morrison, *op. cit.*, p. 99.
[4]*Ibid.*, p. 87.
[5]Powell, *op. cit.*, p. 168.

aside the thought that Paul's 'Powers' are angels."[6] Other writers do not explicitly insist on this Pauline modification. Oscar Cullmann, for example, regularly refers to the Powers as "angels" and "angel powers," but on one occasion he specifically describes them as "almost personified powers,"[7] an indication that he might concur in Berkhof's analysis. In any case, it is unlikely that there is serious disagreement in this area.

There is also an apparent consensus in viewing the influence of the Powers as being manifested in the regular patterns and structures of social life. In discussing this topic, for example, no theologian means to suggest that political leaders are demon-possessed or communing with the spirits in some popular sense of these phrases—as if the Powers operated through direct acts of supernatural intervention. To be sure, it is not always clear as to how the Powers are viewed as exerting their influence; this difficulty, however, is not simply due to defects in current theological understanding but rather to the perils inherent in attempts to duplicate Paul's exact views, given his lack of systematic presentation on the subject.

Let us examine the discussion of the influence of the Powers a little more closely. Morrison tells us that in suggesting a "correspondence"[8] or a "coincidence"[9] between the spirit-world and human decision-making processes, there is "more than an analogy involved" in Paul's thoughts on the subject. Paul sees such a "special close relationship" holding between the two realms that the "rule" involved is to be thought of as "essentially one."[10]

Berkhof sees the Powers as demonstrating their influence in "the structures of earthly existence."[11] As *created* Powers, they were originally intended as "instruments" of God's love for his creation; they are the "weight-bearing

[6]Berkhof, *op. cit.*, p. 19.
[7]Cullmann, *op. cit.*, p. 108.
[8]Morrison, *op. cit.*, p. 22.
[9]*Ibid.*, p. 24.
[10]*Ibid.*, p. 26.
[11]Berkhof, *op. cit.*, p. 18.

substratum of the world," intended by God to serve to "bind men fast in His fellowship."[12] But the Powers presently share in the fallenness of creation; now they are "behaving as though they were the ultimate ground of being."[13] Even under these conditions, however, they continue to "undergird human life and society and preserve them from chaos."[14]

We might think of the Powers, then, as having to do with various forces, spheres, and patterns of our lives which present themselves to us as possible objects of idolatry. Fallen humanity, having chosen to redirect the allegiance that properly belongs to the Creator, turns to various dimensions of the creation in order to find substitute objects of loyalty and trust. Some absolutize a moral code, others a political ideology. A nation or race can become an object of ultimate loyalty, as can sexual enjoyment, humanitarian pursuits, or even a religious commitment. Each of these patterns or forces has been mentioned in the recent literature as relating to a kind of power similar to the Pauline conception. Thus, we are dealing with the domains of the Powers when we are taking an inventory of various possible objects of human idolatry.

We can see, too, how these Powers *could* serve as an aid in ordering human life. None of these things—national or racial grouping, altruism, religious doctrine, moral rules, technology, sexual desire—is in itself a bad thing. They are the patterns and reference points by which we order and regulate our pursuits and decision-making. Without at least some of them, our lives would be chaotic. Properly understood, they can be the Lord's servants, aids in structuring our lives of service and love toward God and neighbor.

Because of our sinful rebellion, however, such matters often take on an additional significance. Our devotion to them becomes an instrument of that rebellion, and we are separated from the love of God. And since such entities as

12*Ibid.*, p. 22.
13*Ibid.*, p. 23.
14*Ibid.*, p. 24.

a nation or a racial group are not morally or ontologically ultimate—so that when we are tempted to offer them our ultimate allegiance we are dealing with "false gods"— human life becomes distorted in its order and direction. The Powers become despotic lords over us. Those spheres of activities and corresponding reference points which were originally intended as means of harmony and partnership now serve as forces of alienation, and lead us finally to ultimate disintegration.

## DISPUTES ABOUT THE POWERS

The preceding account represents what is by now a general consensus about the Pauline references to the Powers. Most recent commentators would agree with the general content of our account thus far; however, some important disagreements emerge when we pursue the topic further.

These disagreements fall into at least three groups. First, there are differences of opinion concerning how many references Paul actually makes to spiritual Powers. Everyone agrees that he did so at certain points. Paul is definitely concerned with the Powers in the letter to the Colossians, and there is little or no dispute over the proper interpretations of, for example, Galatians 4:3, 9, Ephesians 6:12, or Romans 8:38-39. There has been considerable argument, however, over the proper reading of the reference to *archontes* (RSV: "rulers") in I Corinthians 2:8, and to *exousiai* (RSV: "governing authorities") in Romans 13:1. Three choices are possible with respect to the Corinthians passage: (1) Paul was referring *only* to earthly rulers, or (2) *only* to spiritual Powers, or (3) he intended a double reference. The same choices are possible with respect to *exousiai* of Romans 13, although the actual debate in this case has focused on the first and third possibilities.[15]

[15]For a summary of the issues at stake concerning the interpretation of these two passages see Cullmann's excursus on the subject, *op. cit.*, pp. 95ff., and Morrison's precise summary of the arguments on both sides of the question in Part One of his book.

The second area of disagreement has to do with how the redemptive work of Christ affected the status of the Powers. Morrison's position on this question seems least popular: he maintains that the work of Christ "did not change the character or impair the effectiveness of the powers . . . His work was crucial for the liberation of believers from the powers, but apart from that, the authority and rule in this world continued as before."[16] This contention is, according to Markus Barth, unconvincing in the light of Paul's insistence in Colossians 2:15 that Christ "disarmed the principalities and powers."[17] And C. E. B. Cranfield counters Morrison's thesis with this observation:

> While the statement, "When we call the emperor forth to view his new Christological clothes in broad daylight, we find that there are none" [Morrison, p. 116], contains an important truth, since *outwardly* the civil authorities as such have indeed not been affected, it may nevertheless be true to say that an objective change in their situation has been brought about. The issue by a competent authority of a warrant for a man's arrest affects a radical alteration of his situation, even though he and his associates may at the time know nothing about it and may for a while carry on in just the same way as before. And, though it is true that the governments of this world . . . are now no more submissive than they were before, yet the fact that God's claim over them . . . has been decisively and finally asserted, means that they fulfill their functions now under the judgment, mercy and promise of God in a way that was not so before.[18]

The discussion of the actual effects which the death and resurrection of Jesus brought about on the status of the Powers is closely related to the third group of problems, which cluster about the question of how the Christian com-

[16]*Op. cit.*, pp. 118f.
[17]Cf. Markus Barth and Verne H. Fletcher, *Acquittal By Resurrection* (New York: Holt, Rinehart and Winston, 1964), p. 159. Barth's text wrongly identified this verse as "Col. 2:19."
[18]*Op. cit.*, pp. 64f.

munity is to relate to the Powers in the light of Christ's redemptive work. It is not uncommon to find writers on this subject referring to Christ's "defeat" of the Powers, but this claim is usually qualified in important ways. Thus, van den Heuvel writes:

> Although the victory has been wrought the effects still have to be made visible. The powers are unmasked, they are exposed and defeated, but they are not yet brought under the feet of Jesus. The struggle with them goes on.[19]

Berkhof puts it this way:

> The unmasking is actually already their defeat. Yet this is only visible to men when they know that God Himself has appeared on earth in Christ . . . that in Christ God has challenged the Powers, has penetrated their territory, and has displayed that he is stronger than they.[20]

These qualifications point to an important matter concerning the political mission of the church. How ought the Christian community presently to relate to civil authority, knowing that Christ has exposed the Powers and penetrated their territory? We will consider this question in detail shortly, after some further comments concerning the general discussion of the Powers.

## SOME ADDITIONAL PROBLEMS

The body of literature on the Powers, to which we have been referring, constitutes an important development in our understanding of the New Testament. However, our grasp of this significant Pauline theme cannot be judged complete or satisfactory on the basis of the recent discussion. In addition to those above-mentioned matters which may not have been resolved to date, even after lengthy debate, the dis-

[19]*Op. cit.,* p. 46.
[20]*Op. cit.,* p. 31.

cussion of the Powers raises further questions and problems which have received little or no attention in the existing literature. We must list a few of these items here, not because we are going to pursue them in the present discussion, but for the purpose of placing them on the theological agenda.

First, it is characteristic of discussions of the Powers that writers will begin by describing the scope of the topic in very general terms. We are told, for example, that these forces "regulate" the courses of the planets, moral codes, technological activity, educational patterns, sexual pursuits, racial and ethnic allegiances, and the like. Yet the application of the theme is almost always with respect to the political realm. This need not be viewed as a defect—especially if there is reason to think that attaining clarity with regard to the political applications will provide us with a basis for extending the discussion to other areas. If writers on this topic are correct that an understanding of the Powers is *crucial,* then it is also crucial for Christian participation in educational institutions, technological developments, "personal" ethical pursuits, and the like. An application of the discussion to these and other areas would seem critically important for the guidance of the Christian community. Deserving of special note in this regard is the question of what the Pauline texts mean for the contemporary church's message to those who have in effect revived some pagan themes popular in Paul's day. Popular fascination with astrology, Eastern religion, demon-possession and related phenomena seems to indicate that a fuller understanding of the principalities and powers can make an important contribution to the task of evangelism.

Second, we need a clearer sorting out of the differences between the Pauline Powers and the forces of "chaos" which also appear in the biblical drama. The need for clarification in this area can be demonstrated by considering an example. Throughout the Scriptures "the waters" often serve as a means of symbolizing chaotic and destructive forces somehow present in the creation. Psalm 93 pictures the Creator as "mightier than the thunders of many waters," even though "the floods have lifted up their voice" as a challenge to the Lord's greatness (see vv. 3-4). Furthermore, this kind of reference in the Psalms points us in two temporal directions. When Israel sang about God's encounters with the "waters" it was probably with the memory of such events as the ordering of the chaotic waters at creation (Gen. 1:6), the unleashing of the "fountains of the great deep" and the opening of the "windows of heaven" in judgment at the time of the deluge (Gen. 7:11), and the parting of the waters for the purpose of deliverance from Egypt (Exod. 14:21). But for the Christian community the portrayals of God's encounters with the "waters" point forward to Christ's calming of the sea (Mark 4:39), as well as to the age that is yet to come, when the angry waters—which in the apocalyptic literature are pictured as presently spewing forth raging beasts bent on destruction—will become "as it were a sea of glass," beside which stand beasts singing doxologies to God (Rev. 4:6-8).

Our question is: How are we to understand the role of the Powers in these pictures? On one reading, the Powers are forces created by God to guard the creation *against* the forces of chaos. But the Powers are *themselves* often described as destructive forces pitted against the rule of God. Have they become, as "rebellious Powers," aligned with the threat of chaos? Or are they still guarding against that threat, but posing a distinct threat of their own at the same time? To be more specific in our question: When Jesus stilled the waves, was the turbulent sea functioning as an instrument of the Powers who were then stilled by Jesus? Or was Jesus *harnessing* the Powers as a means of confronting a chaotic threat distinct from the Powers?

Third, it is not always clear from discussions of the Powers how we are to distinguish one Power from another. Berkhof tells us that in Hitler's Germany "the powers of *Volk*, race and state took a new grip on men."[21] Are we to

[21]Rauschenbusch, *A Theology for the Social Gospel* (New York: Macmillan, 1918), p. 243.

understand this as a situation in which *three* Powers were operating, or was Nazism a *single* Power using at least three factors? Similarly, in a struggle between races is a single Power—race—operating or two "race-Powers?" How many Powers are in operation at the United Nations? Is it proper to think of one Power as acting in opposition to another Power?

These are not intended as idle or facetious questions. Each of the three problems we have raised—as well as our next item—points to the desirability of developing an "ontology" of the Powers. It may be that such an account, while desirable, is not possible to develop in any detail. At the very least, it would have to be based on some extrabiblical speculation. But without the formulation of at least some ontological principles of this sort, the theology of the Powers will necessarily remain vague and—at certain crucial points—unhelpful as an instrument of Christian discernment.

Fourth, it would help if we could be clearer about how far we may legitimately interpret Paul's references to Powers as involving personification, especially since some of the passages in which the Powers appear contain other references which he probably intended to be taken in that way—for example, the references to "death," "height," and "depth" in Romans 8:38-39. Did Paul really think that in speaking of Powers he was referring to distinct entities which operated as causal factors with respect to human affairs? And if he did, are *we* required to posit the existence of such entities?

One does not need to be enamored of the enterprise of demythologizing to insist on the importance of these questions. Indeed, a concern with them is indispensable for anyone who dissents from the motives of the demythologizers. If we are going to take the Pauline message seriously we must attempt to clarify its meaning, as he intended it, as well as to sort out the ways in which it can be usefully employed by the church today. If we assume that what Paul is saying in these references is both true and helpful, we cannot avoid asking *how* it is true and how it is helpful. Was Paul insisting on the correctness of some key elements of the widely accepted cosmology of his day? Or was he merely employing the language of this cosmology as figures of speech? In what legitimate manner can we speak this way today? As personification and metaphor? As intended references to "spiritual agents"? As "reified" social attitudes and forces?

Along these lines it is interesting to examine perspectives in Christian political thought formulated before the recent interest in the Pauline "principalities and powers." As an example, Walter Rauschenbusch's writings exhibit at times a strong desire to purge Christian social thought of biblical themes that depend on "the semi-dualistic religion of the Empire and the prevalent belief in the rule of demons." But Rauschenbusch also observes at one point that there is a "blood-kin" relationship between "the ancient demonic conception and the modern social conviction."[22] The demonic conception, for Rauschenbusch, was a healthy one when it was a means of sensitizing the Christian community to the existence of "oppressive international forces" whose designs could not be explained merely in terms of the decisions of distinct individuals.[23]

Thus Rauschenbusch himself can observe that Jesus was crucified, not just by individuals, but by such "constitutional forces in the Kingdom of Evil" as "religious bigotry, the combination of graft and political power, the corruption of justice, the mob spirit, militarism, and class contempt."[24] Given that Rauschenbusch understands these forces along the lines of Josiah Royce's conception of "super-personal forces in human life,"[25] to what degree was he approximating the Pauline conception, even without the benefit of recent scholarship on the subject? There are numerous ways of analyzing a claim like "Jesus was crucified by religious

[22]*Ibid.*, p. 87.
[23]*Ibid.*, pp. 88f.
[24]*Ibid.*, pp. 257f.
[25]As he admits, *ibid.*, pp. 70-71.

bigotry" as a *true* claim—including, in addition to Royce's metaphysics, the kinds of analyses that might be offered by Marx or Durkheim. Which of these are permitted, or ruled out, on the basis of Pauline thought? Does Paul's view commit us to the belief that there is an "ontological" or "causal" residue that exists "over and above" observable individual and sociological factors? These questions, as well as the others we have raised, deserve to be submitted to careful reflection and research.

## THE POWERS AND POLITICAL INVOLVEMENT

Assuming that much of the recent discussion of the Powers is important and beneficial for the Christian community's political deliberations—and none of the foregoing is meant to cast doubt on that assumption—what are the implications of this discussion for what we have called kingly involvement in the political order? On this subject, too, there seems to be disagreement among those who have written about the Powers, although the differences are not always openly addressed.

Let us consider the different emphases we find in the discussions of Berkhof and John H. Yoder. Toward the end of his discussion Berkhof speaks favorably of possible attempts at a "Christianization" of the Powers.

> But we must be cautious with the word ["Christianization"]. It can mean no more than that the Powers, instead of being ideological centers, are what God meant them to be: helps, instruments, giving shape and direction to the genuine life of man as child of God and as neighbor.
>
> That they are "Christianized" means they are made instrumental, made modest; one could even say "neutralized." . . . For the state it means "de-ideologizing," a reduction to its true dimensions. The state no longer serves its own interest and no longer enslaves men to the world view it propagates; it becomes simply a means of staving off chaos and ordering human relations in such a way that

we can lead a quiet and stable life and follow God's call, unhampered by external hindrances.[26]

The comparison of this kind of perspective with Yoder's views is interesting for a number of reasons. For one thing, the differences between Berkhof's and Yoder's applications of the discussion of the Powers to the question of Christian attitudes toward the civil order are representative of some of the classic disagreements between Reformed and Anabaptist thought. Furthermore, Berkhof's work was translated into English by Yoder, and Yoder refers favorably to this work on a regular basis in his own writing, although it seems obvious that he would strongly disagree with important elements in Berkhof's call for a "Christianization" of the Powers. Perhaps most significant is the fact that Berkhof's remarks on this subject are typical of many of those who write on the Powers, in that they assume few difficulties in finding a proper form of Christian involvement in the domain of the Powers. Yoder's discussion is much more detailed and precise on this subject, and it merits close examination.

## THE ANABAPTIST-REFORMED DIALOGUE

Before looking at some of the details of Yoder's discussion, some note must be taken of the historical setting in which we are examining his views. Discussion between the Reformed and Anabaptist communities on matters of politics—to which the following pages are meant as a contribution—is an urgent necessity in the contemporary ecumenical setting. In the Christian community as a whole, and especially within "conservative evangelical" borders, the political differences between these two perspectives bring many current tensions into bold relief.[27]

[26]Berkhof, op. cit., pp. 49f.
[27]For further comments on the current tensions between Anabaptist and Reformed perspectives on political matters — especially as they pertain to contemporary evangelical discussions — see Marlin Van Elderen, "Evangelicals and Liberals: Is There a Common

There is also every reason to think that the Anabaptist-Reformed dialogue can be carried on more profitably today than was often possible in the past. Reformed Christians must admit that many of the political ventures of the past associated with Calvinism have been, as the Anabaptists have insisted, "Constantinian" and misguided. (Yoder may have overstated the case when he observed—at a 1974 Conference on Christianity and Politics at Calvin College—that Jesus' resistance to the third temptation in the wilderness was in effect a refusal to become a "Calvinist"; but there can be no doubt that some Reformed Christians have been less firm than their Lord was in dealing with the Devil on this point.)

The potential for fruitful discussion becomes even more apparent from a reading of Yoder's works. *The Politics of Jesus* adds significantly to our understanding of the political message of the New Testament. Our critical remarks below will focus on a rather small portion of the message of that book. Furthermore, while some of Yoder's themes in *The Politics of Jesus* may strike Reformed readers as having an anti-political tone, a careful attempt to view this work in the larger context of his published work[28] will reveal that one of Yoder's major concerns has been to prod his Mennonite constituency into those areas of responsible political involvement which are compatible with the Anabaptist understanding of discipleship. In short, Yoder's scholarly efforts have made the Reformed-Anabaptist discussion easier to pursue, and even though that discussion will necessarily involve some argument on either side there can be no doubt that the argument takes place in mutual awe before the cross of Christ.

We will examine three closely related themes in Yoder's discussion, each of which have an important bearing

Ground?", *Christianity and Crisis* (July 18, 1974), pp. 153-155; and also my "Weaving a Coherent Pattern of Discipleship," *Christian Century* (Aug. 20-27, 1975), pp. 730-731.

[28]See, for example, Yoder's *The Christian Witness to the State* (Newton, Kansas, 1964).

on the question of political involvement: (1) Yoder's concept of "revolutionary subordination"; (2) his views of the proper mode of Christian moral and political decision-making; and (3) his account of the manner in which believers ought to "imitate" the work of Christ on the cross.

## "REVOLUTIONARY SUBORDINATION"

"Revolutionary subordination," Yoder's description of the proper Christian posture toward the civil order, can be understood in terms of the partial analogy that he draws between the kind of advice Paul gives to women and slaves and the manner in which Paul advises Christians to relate to the state. Paul's advice to women and slaves, in 1 Corinthians and elsewhere, would not be necessary, Yoder surmises (and rightly so), if they had not already been realizing the liberating power of the gospel which eradicates the patterns of domination and submission. Since they are realizing their true worth in Christ, Paul is telling them, they should not waste their efforts in attempts to change the patterns of the larger society. Their

> freedom can already be realized within [the] present status by voluntarily accepting subordination, in view of the relative unimportance of such social distinctions when seen in the light of the coming fulfillment of God's purposes.[29]

This same advice would seem to hold for the Christian's relationship to the civil order, with one important difference. When Paul offers advice to women and slaves he also issues a call for husbands and masters to conform to patterns of servanthood. But there is no analogous

> invitation to the king to conceive of himself as a public servant. Was this only because, as a matter of course, the apostolic preachers and authors recognized that there were not kings in their audiences? Or was it that, in line with

[29]*The Politics of Jesus,* p. 187.

the teaching of Christ, which had been preserved in several forms, Jesus had instructed his disciples specifically to reject governmental domination over others as unworthy of the disciple's calling of servanthood?[30]

Yoder accepts the latter alternative; it is precisely because the Christian rejects "governmental domination" that he can be subordinate to such domination, accepting the obligations of "the voluntary subordination of one who knows that another regime is normative."[31] The adopting of this posture involves "accepting powerlessness," as well as the refusal to exercise "brute power" or "violent lordship" or to promote "righteousness backed by power" as a part of the vain attempt to "govern history."

Yoder's "revolutionary subordination," then, involves an attitude of ambivalence toward civil government. Christians must in some sense approve of government. This approval seems to operate on at least two levels. Whatever the merits or demerits of a given political rule, we must submit to it because God has commanded us to do so. The required "subjection" to government does not necessarily involve moral approval of governmental policies nor obedience to every governmental dictate: "The conscientious objector who refuses to do what his government asks him to do, but still remains under the sovereignty of that government and accepts the penalties which it imposes . . . is being subordinate even though he is not obeying."[32] On this level, then, Christian approval includes a toleration of the existence of government—a refusal to engage in "revolution or insubordination," even against tyrannical governments,[33] out of a willingness to participate "in the character of God's victorious patience with the rebellious powers of his creation."[34]

On a second, more specific, level, it is possible for Chris-

[30]*Ibid.*, p. 188.
[31]*Ibid.*, p. 192.
[32]*Ibid.*, p. 212.
[33]*Ibid.*, p. 204.
[34]*Ibid.*, p. 213.

tian approval of government to be directed toward actual functions performed by governments. There is a broad sense in which whatever a government does is providentially ordered by God; this, however, does not mean that whatever a government does is good. But there are some governmental functions which can be labeled as good by Christians, albeit in a modest sense. These functions have to do with maintaining peace and order in a limited manner (the police function), which is subject to certain safeguards.[35]

We referred above to Yoder's understanding of Christian discipleship as including a rejection of "governmental domination over others." It should be clear by now that we ought not to interpret him as thereby calling for a simple rejection of government. The Christian must share in God's providential patience with governments, however tyrannical; he must also hope for governments who will promote social harmony without committing gross injustices in the process. Furthermore, Yoder should not even be understood as ruling out some degree of participation in government. In *The Christian Witness to the State* Yoder suggests that involvement in the elective process can be an important means by which Christians "speak to those in authority." Indeed, *refusal* to vote, if it is to be justified on Christian grounds, should be construed as a means of positive witness.[36] It is even conceivable that a "legislator, if he has no concern for his re-election or for developing a power bloc, could without compromise conceive of his office more as an occasion to speak to the authorities than as being an agent of government."[37]

We can see where the *ambivalence* toward government lies for Yoder. "Patience" with governments does not mean a lack of concern about governmental policies; Yoder is not advocating a quietistic posture of withdrawal. This concern, however, cannot take the form of involvement,

[35]*Ibid.*, p. 206; see also *The Christian Witness to the State,* pp. 36f.
[36]*The Christian Witness to the State*, p. 27.
[37]*Ibid.*, p. 28.

because the political order operates in accordance with patterns incompatible with Christian discipleship. So, the Christian must "speak to authorities"; but a Christian can never operate as "an agent of government."

Within this framework, Yoder's argument with Calvinists has to do with far more than the question of pacifism and the legitimacy of just war considerations. On the Calvinist view, as he understands it, "what is ordained is not a particular government but the concept of proper government, the principle of government as such." The Calvinist claims to possess criteria for distinguishing between proper and improper governments; so,

> if . . . a government fails adequately to fulfill the functions divinely assigned to it, it loses its authority. It then becomes the duty of the preacher to teach that this has become an unjust government, worthy of rebellion. It can become the duty of Christian citizens to rise up against it, not because they are against government but because they are in favor of *proper* government.[38]

As over against this view, which assumes the legitimacy of "the integral distinction between good governments, which Christians should bless, and bad ones against which they should rebel," Yoder insists that Christians "should rather rebel against all and be subordinate to all; for 'subordination' is itself the Christian form of rebellion. It is the way we share in God's patience with a system we basically reject."[39]

It is important to note here the matters on which Yoder does *not* disagree with the Calvinist. He does not deny that there is *some* kind of distinction to be made between proper and improper government: "There are criteria that come into play in our attitude towards government. . . . The place of government in the providential designs of God is not such that our duty would be simply to do whatever it

[38]*The Politics of Jesus*, p. 201.
[39]*Ibid.*, p. 202 n. 10.

says."[40] And he would agree with the Calvinist that the Christian is provided with a basis for offering an aggressive critique of specific governmental policies—a critique which might even be presented through some kind of use of political channels.

The important points of disagreement are as follows. First, Yoder would reject the Calvinist's *basis* for deriving norms for distinguishing between proper and improper governmental activity. Second, he would reject as improper some items which the Calvinist would place within the proper domain of governmental activity. And, third, he would dissent from Calvinist prescriptions concerning the motivation for and manner of political involvement.

In order to be clear about the roots of some of these disagreements, let us briefly sketch out some of the considerations the Calvinist would want to introduce at this point. Our first consideration was touched on in an earlier chapter. Are we to view human governments as essentially coercive and manipulative, or are these elements of governmental activity connected only with the functioning of government under sinful conditions? If the latter is the case (as many Calvinists have argued), we already possess a rudimentary grasp, by virtue of the distinction between sinless and sinful government, of proper and improper governmental activity. (Of course, on this distinction it is still necessary to distinguish between activities and policies which *result from* the sinfulness of governments and those which are appropriate governmental responses to the sinfulness of human beings as such.)

This line of argument is closely associated with the "theocratic" ideal which Yoder rightly sees as operating in the Calvinist tradition.[41] Calvinists and Anabaptists would agree that Old Testament Israel and the New Testament church are "theocratic" societies. The question is whether it is proper to attempt to bring contemporary societies (in

[40]*Ibid.*, p. 211.
[41]See *The Christian Witness to the State*, pp. 64f.

addition, that is, to the contemporary church) into some degree of conformity to theocratic standards.

The Calvinist insistence that such attempts are legitimate (and even mandatory) is based on an argument which involves several steps. First, there is the background assumption that the political dimensions of human society are not merely post-fall phenomena. If, as we argued earlier, the human race had "multiplied" to a significant degree even *without* the entrance of sin into human affairs, some form of human government would have been necessary— although not a form characterized by the coercive patterns associated with sin. Furthermore, the maintenance of this kind of governmental activity would have been a legitimate extension of the mandate to have dominion.

Second, the Calvinist would want to point to the kinds of accommodations to the sinful condition that take place within the kind of theocratic framework which develops even after the fall. When Samuel brought the request of the elders of Israel, who wanted a human king, before the Lord, the divine response was initially one of a disapproval of the motivation for that request: "Hearken to the voice of the people in all that they say to you; for they have not rejected you, but they have rejected me from being king over them" (1 Sam. 8:7). But the shift from a purer theocracy to one of administration by human kings does not completely obliterate the promise of divine guidance and blessing. Indeed, there seems to be a divine accommodation to the change of government, as is indicated in Samuel's subsequent speech to Israel: "If you will fear the Lord and serve him and hearken to his voice and not rebel against the commandment of the Lord, and if both you and the king who reigns over you will follow the Lord your God, it will be well" (1 Sam. 12:14).

The songs of Israel reflect this desire for a divine blessing on human rule, even to the point that the king is often viewed as a very important channel of divine blessing:

Give the king thy justice, O God,

and thy righteousness to the royal son!
May he judge thy people with righteousness,
and thy poor with justice!
Let the mountains bring prosperity for the people,
and the hills in righteousness!
May he defend the cause of the poor of the people,
give deliverance to the needy,
and crush the oppressor! (Ps. 72:1-4)

The next step in the argument is important, since one could argue that this line of reasoning assumes a theocratic context, so that the attitudes toward human rulers in a theocracy—whether pre- or post-lapsarian—are irrelevant to nontheocratic contexts. But it is a fact that in the Old Testament there *are* attempts—on the part of those who presuppose a theocratic base of operation—to address pagan political situations. Thus, Amos does not restrict his prophetic critique to Israelite policies (ch. 1); Jeremiah counsels the Israelites in captivity to "seek the welfare of the city where I have sent you into exile, and pray to the Lord on its behalf, for in its welfare you will find your welfare" (29:7); and Daniel admonishes Nebuchadnezzar to "break of your sins by practicing righteousness and your iniquities by showing mercy to the oppressed, that there may perhaps be a lengthening of your tranquility" (4:27).

In each of these Old Testament examples there seems to be an extension of at least some of the principles learned in a theocratic context to nontheocratic political situations. These individuals seem to make the transition from the expectation that justice will be promoted in the midst of a redeemed people to the insistence that those same standards of justice can be applied even where the God of Israel is not acknowledged as Lord.

The Reformed Christian is willing to take the argument a step further. When the New Testament church offered "supplications, prayers, intercessions, and thanksgiving . . . for all men, for kings and all who are in high positions" (1 Tim. 2:1-2), this was done in continuity with the Old Testament vision of a righteous society, the standards for

which could even be applied to pagan rulers. On this interpretation, it is not unthinkable that some Christians might
go beyond praying for justice. Should the opportunity arise,
as it did in the Old Testament for Joseph and Daniel, they
might even seize the chance to promote justice by serving
in pagan courts.

## THE REFUSAL TO "MANAGE SOCIETY"

The foregoing is not enough to cast conclusive doubts
on Yoder's concept of "revolutionary subordination." It could
be replied that, while there may be some surface plausibility to the Calvinist reading of the biblical situation, we
have failed to touch on the crux of the issue. Thus far, we
have a situation in which the Reformed perspective is, at
best, a plausible alternative to the Anabaptist position. But,
it might be argued, the plausibility fades in the light of
further considerations. More specifically, we must come to
grips with Yoder's contention that the New Testament
thrusts on us a pattern of decision-making which stands as
a radical alternative to that which inspires attempts to "manage society" or to promote "righteousness backed by power."

Yoder singles out what he views as three widely accepted, but false, assumptions in Christian social ethics: (1)
the presumption that "the relationship of cause and effect
is visible, understandable, and manageable, so that if we
make our choice on the basis of how we hope society will
be moved, it will be moved in that direction"; (2) the
assumption that we "are adequately informed to be able
to set for ourselves and for all society the goal toward
which we seek to move it"; and (3) an assumption even
more basic than the other two: "that effectiveness in moving
toward these goals which have been set is itself a moral
yardstick."[42]

Let us apply this to a concrete example. Imagine that
a group of Christians is concerned about poor housing standards in the slum areas of a large city. Suppose these Chris-

[42]*The Politics of Jesus,* p. 235.

tians were to band together for the purpose of pressuring politicians into concern about this problem, formulating potential legislation, and working to elect persons who will carry out their wishes. Not everything about this would be misguided on Yoder's view; we must keep in mind his stress on the importance of "speaking to those in authority." What he would consider wrongheaded is purportedly Christian action which assumed the legitimacy of the premises cited above. Thus it would be wrong to presuppose that (1) we have the kind of evidence necessary to be certain that we can move the political process toward the housing-legislation goals that we posit; (2) that we have a reasonable basis for positing the goals themselves as the morally proper ones to seek; and (3) that our effectiveness in reaching such goals is a morally proper criterion for action.

As Christians, Yoder holds, we must not ask how we can cause good things to happen but how we can act in such a way that our actions witness to God's *already having acted decisively* in the cross of Jesus Christ. How can we act as those whose actions are the *effects* of what God has brought about on the cross? We must, as Yoder put it in a recent article, "see our obedience more as praising God, and less as running His world for Him."[43]

There are several difficulties which can be raised with respect to Yoder's perspective on Christian decision-making. First, the refusal to "run God's world for him," or to "manage society," is not a posture whose praiseworthiness is immediately obvious. How does it relate to the biblical mandate for human beings to "have dominion" in the created order? If human beings are created with the capacity for assessing situations, projecting into the future, planning strategies, and the like, would it not seem a judicious exercise of created abilities to put these gifts to use, even in the area of social and political planning? And if God does require us to do these things, some attempts to "run his world for him" might be an important means of praising him.

Second, while it is indeed important to warn ourselves—

43"The Biblical Mandate," *Post-American* (April 1974), p. 25.

as Yoder effectively encourages us to do—that we must not view other human beings as completely "locked into" a deterministrically understood cause-and-effect process, we must be careful not to carry this warning to the extreme. We must, indeed, guard against assuming an attitude of omniscience, but we must also be warned against retreating to an attitude of skepticism. Calculation and prediction are crucial elements in our everyday experience, and they are even important in our interpersonal and social maneuverings. Without them it would be very difficult to walk through a crowd or drive a car down a busy street.

No moral theory can ignore the crucial importance of prediction and calculation without risking unintelligibility. Suppose a person was considering telling a joke about a funeral—one which it would be perfectly proper to tell under many circumstances, but not in the presence of people who were experiencing grief over the recent loss of a family member. The telling of this joke, then, would in this situation act as a causal factor in bringing about unnecessary offense. A human being can only decide this by calculating probable reactions, projecting cause-and-effect patterns, and evaluating the effects of specific actions. To insist on this account of moral decision-making is not necessarily to accept a crass utilitarianism. Rather, it is to recognize something that is indispensable for any kind of moral deliberation: in order to know the morally relevant features of a situation we must get our facts straight, which regularly involves predicting the responses and reactions of human beings to specific courses of action.

Third, it is important to make a distinction between engaging in actions that will have the effect of coercing other human beings and acting out of a desire to coerce and dominate others. All Christians should hope to be delivered from the latter pattern, since the desire to dominate and coerce is closely related to the sinful project that began with the serpent's lie, "You shall be as gods."

Yoder would argue, however, that it is the rejection of the former—and broader—pattern, thereby eschewing *all* coercion, which distinguishes a truly Christian life-style from all other forms of human interaction. There can be no doubt that the refusal to engage in any coercion-producing actions would introduce a very different pattern into human affairs. What it would not do, however, is to introduce a new pattern into politics, since the avoidance of all coercion-producing activity is, in effect, a rejection of significant political activity.

Our more limited alternative—the rejection of actions that flow simply from a desire to coerce others—has the advantage, then, of allowing for a new departure within the political arena. Such a departure would be realized if Christians pursued political activity with a desire to promote justice coupled with a genuine love of neighbor and humility before God.

We must also note that the concepts of coercion, violence, and domination are not always easy to explicate clearly. In the ecclesiastical community and in the family, matters of church discipline and child-rearing often pose problematic situations in which coercion—even violence— seems unavoidable. It may be that the lessons that Christians learn in these more personal areas can be transformed, by extension, into more just political practices.

Furthermore, it is not clear that the Christian who refuses to act to curb political or economic oppression thereby escapes responsibility for coercion and domination. The refusal to act can be, on occasion—especially when there is some evidence that our actions might succeed—itself a way of "managing the affairs of others"; inaction can sometimes be as brutal as action.

Once again, none of this provides a decisive case against Yoder's position. Indeed, it is likely that he would interpret some of our concerns as proper warnings against potential distortions of his own perspective. What we have attempted to gain here, however, is a clearer focus on where the crucial issues lie. We can agree with Yoder that it is wrong to attempt to "manage God's world" in improper ways. We are agreed that we ought not to try to "make things happen" which ought *not* to happen. And we concur in his insistence that the Christian has no business harboring desires to dominate and coerce.

This brings us to the final point that we will examine in Yoder's case. Here we face the question that is fundamental to all the rest: What kinds of actions, if any, are compatible with the commitments of those who are living in grateful response to what God did in the cross of Jesus Christ? Here, too, the question is not whether we view our actions as constituting a response to the work of the cross. In spite of the way in which Yoder occasionally formulates the matter, the difference between the Anabaptist and the Calvinist is not that the former views his activity as an "effect" of the cross, whereas the latter wants to "cause things to happen." The question is: What kinds of actions are proper effects of the cross?

## "ACCEPTING POWERLESSNESS"

The crucial factor in Yoder's answer to the question of Christian political involvement is his understanding of the confrontation with the Powers which took place in the death and resurrection of Jesus Christ. On his account the proper Christian posture toward the civil order cannot be decided on the basis of a theocratic conception or an appeal to general political obligations. However legitimate the inclination to engage in governmental domination may seem, and however laudable attempts to manage society may appear on the basis of other considerations, these patterns must finally be judged in the light of the cross of Christ.

In the work of the cross, Yoder argues, Christ wrought a victory over "the powers" in a manner which would count from any other perspective as a defeat. Christ confronted the powers by "accepting powerlessness":

> The Powers have been defeated not by some kind of cosmic hocus-pocus but by the concreteness of the cross; the impact of the cross upon them is not the working of magi-

**111**

cal words nor the fulfillment of a legal contract calling for the shedding of innocent blood, but the sovereign presence, within the structures of creaturely orderliness, of Jesus the kingly claimant and of the church who herself is a structure and a power in society.[44]

The Christian's submission to the state grows out of an attempt to imitate the work of Christ on the cross, a work characterized by "the voluntary subordination of one who knows that another regime is normative."[45]

Yoder rightly rejects traditional "romantic" versions of the call to "imitate Christ"—which have been characteristic, oddly enough, of both liberal and fundamentalist emphases on a "What would Jesus do?" style of decision-making. There are many things which Jesus did which it would be simply wrong for us to attempt to imitate: it would be foolish, for example, to try to catch a departing boat by trying to walk on the water, and it would be highly improper for any of us to describe himself as the Son of man. For Yoder, the imitation of Christ must center on the work of the cross: "Only at one point, only on one subject—but then *consistently, universally*—is Jesus our example: in his cross."[46]

The "consistently [and] universally" modifier is the crucial one here. This is why, for Yoder, it is absolutely clear that to participate in "the Lamb's war" means that Christians must refuse to "manage society." Jesus confronted the Powers by refusing to follow their pattern of exercising "violent lordship"; his "revolutionary subordination" *was* the mode of his victory over the Powers. We too, then, must "accept powerlessness" in order to claim "participation in the character of God's victorious patience with the rebellious powers of his creation."[47]

Our critical response to Yoder's case on this point will consist in the support of a counterclaim: namely, that we *cannot* "consistently and universally" imitate the work of the

[44]*The Politics of Jesus*, p. 162.
[45]*Ibid.*, p. 192.
[46]*Ibid.*, p. 97, italics added.
[47]*Ibid.*, p. 213.

cross. The counterclaim will be explained by way of three observations.

First, Yoder does not seem to be quite accurate in describing the confrontation with the Powers as if it were a fully "visible" event. The encounter with the forces of evil seems to involve more than can be grasped by viewing the historical concreteness of the cross. By observing the events of Golgotha, even in the light of Easter morning, we do not see all that is significant about the transaction that took place on the cross. This is because when we refer to the work of the cross we are pointing to an event that has important links to both previous and later ones: these events include, in addition to the resurrection, the temptations in the wilderness, the lifetime of involvement on Jesus' part in our sinful condition, the agony in Gethsemane, the ascension to the Father, and the final act of putting all enemies under his feet.

There is much in the complex redemptive transaction, of which the cross is the focal point, that seems mysterious. If the term "hocus pocus" is to be brought in at this point, we must insist that even this crude term points in the direction of a legitimate element in the complex work of redemption. When all of this complexity is taken into account, we can legitimately ask to what degree we are to imitate certain aspects of the suffering of Jesus, in view of the fact that his suffering had connections to events that we cannot duplicate.

Second—and this observation is closely related to the previous one—it is interesting that Yoder describes Jesus' relationship to the Powers as one of "subordination," a term traditionally used also to describe his relationship to God the Father. This latter notion of subordination, applying to Jesus' obedience to the will of the Father, has been closely related to an understanding of the cross as a payment for sin.

It should be made clear that when we view the cross as a transaction with the Powers, we do not need to do so in such a way that we abandon our understanding of the cross as a quasi-legal economic transaction. Van den Heuvel rightly points out that Paul does not neglect this latter emphasis, even when he is explicitly discussing the confrontation with the Powers. In Colossians 2:13-15, where Paul writes of the triumph over the Powers, he prefaces this with the announcement that God has "forgiven us all our trespasses, having cancelled the bond which stood against us, . . . nailing it to the cross."

An appreciation of the theology of the Powers does not need to dull our enthusiasm for the proclamation that "Jesus paid it all." Indeed, the future hymn of the saints, as recorded in Revelation 5:9-10, suggests the integral relationship between the payment aspect of the cross and the encounter with the Powers:

> Worthy art thou to take the scroll and to open its seals,
> for thou wast slain and by thy blood didst ransom men
> for God from every tribe and tongue and people and nation,
> and hast made them a kingdom and priests to our God,
> and they shall reign on earth.

By his death on the cross Jesus Christ has paid the ransom in order to reconcile us with God. And by that same act he overcame the Powers in order to establish a new kingdom in which we can reign with him. It is not even quite accurate, then, to say that there were *two* things going on at the cross: a "subordination" to the Father and a submission to the Powers. In an important sense the payment for sin *required* a victory over the Powers, and the encounter with the Powers was an *element* in the offering of the ransom. Without the confrontation with the "principalities and powers," it would not be possible to proclaim that "Jesus paid it *all!*"

Finally, it is not only a matter of theological technicality, but a cause for great personal comfort for Christians to know that they need not consistently and universally imitate the death of Jesus. In his well-known essay on the differences between the Greek view of immortality and the biblical teaching regarding the resurrection of the body, Oscar Cullmann effectively draws a stark contrast between the death of Socrates and the death of Jesus.[48] As the scene is recorded in Plato's *Phaedo*, Socrates faces his impending death with great serenity. He calmly chats with his friends, and even chides them for regretting the fact that he must die; finally, he takes the hemlock in happy anticipation of a better world. Jesus, on the other hand, faces his death with horror and agony, pleading with his disciples to keep the watch with him, and begging the Father, with sweat-drops of blood, to let the cup pass from him. Finally, on the cross he cries out as one who has been forsaken by the Father.

We do not have to face death as Jesus did. Indeed, there is no obvious impropriety in the spectacle of a follower of Jesus who faces death more after the manner of Socrates. For Jesus was not simply facing death; he was facing an encounter with sin and death that no human being before or since need face. He had *the* encounter with death; his agony was proper because he was about to remove the curse of death. Because he accomplished that, we can proclaim—as he could not, either in Gethsemane or on the cross—"O Death, where is thy sting?"

If it would be wrong for us to think that we must face death in the way Jesus did, why must we face the Powers after the manner of his work on the cross? His was *the* confrontation with the Powers—the means of their ultimate defeat. On the cross their sting too was removed. We do not have to fear them because of Christ's encounter with them. Just as we need not submit helplessly to death, so we can now enter the domains of the Powers, seeking to promote justice and righteousness, in the confidence that they cannot separate us from God's love. Or so it would seem.

For the reasons given, then, we must disagree with

[48]Oscar Cullmann, "Immortality of the Soul or Resurrection of the Dead: The Witness of the New Testament," reprinted, among others, in *Immortality*, ed. Terence Penelhum (Belmont, Calif.: Wadsworth, 1973), pp. 60-63.

Yoder's insistence that we imitate the cross "consistently, universally." And if there are no convincing *general* grounds for arguing that the Christian must imitate the cross in the manner Yoder suggests, some further argument must be given before we accept his specific recommendations concerning the Christian imitation of Jesus' encounter with the Powers.

However, even though we must reject Yoder's specific recommendations, we do not mean to deny the power and profundity of the Christian vision he articulates. If Reformed Christians, and their political fellow-travelers among the faithful, are going to emphasize the legitimacy of Christian involvement in political structures, it must be with an Anabaptist-type conviction that the Christian disciple must walk in a new and better way. The question cannot be *whether* all Christians must fight "the Lamb's war," but rather *how* we shall do so. And there is perhaps no better opportunity for Christian political activists to struggle with this question than to permit their sensitivities to be molded and corrected by the kind of perspective Yoder offers.

# CHAPTER SIX

# POLITICS AND THE COMING KINGDOM

In his recent book on the subject of death, Russell Aldwinckle begins his discussion with a chapter entitled "Last Things First."[1] By placing our own treatment of eschatological themes at the end of our discussion, we do not mean to be casting a vote against Aldwinckle's important prescription. Eschatology has an integral relationship to the rest of theology. It deals with the creation as *restored,* sin as *eliminated,* and redemption as *completed.* Thus, no perspective on creation or sin or redemption will be fully adequate if it is devoid of eschatological references.

The subject of eschatology is a large one, and we cannot hope to do justice to its scope here. But at least we must raise, by way of concluding our discussion of politics in the biblical drama, questions about the ultimate fate of the political order as we now experience it in the light of biblical visions of "last things."

Our own answer to the questions about the fate of the political order will be developed in critical response to two alternative perspectives—the position of dispensationalist

[1]Russell Aldwinckle, *Death in the Secular City* (Grand Rapids: Eerdmans, 1974), Chapter One.

fundamentalism and the attitudes associated with those "radical" Christians who view the current political order as a manifestation of demonic "Babylonian" patterns.

## DISPENSATIONALIST "ISRAEL-MONISM"

Fundamentalist Christianity is regularly described as an apolitical religion. This characterization is seriously defective, in the light of the prevalence of dispensationalist theology among fundamentalists. According to dispensationalism, God has two distinct redemptive plans in operation, with respect to two different redemptive entities, Israel and the church. As Lewis Sperry Chafer puts it:

> The all-too-common practice of imposing Christianity back upon Judaism or Judaism forward upon Christianity, is the cause of that dire confusion which appears in some theological literature. The Word of God distinguishes between earth and heaven, even after they are created new. Similarly and as clearly it distinguishes between God's consistent and eternal earthly purpose, which is the substance of Judaism; and His consistent and eternal heavenly purpose which is the substance of Christianity, and it is as illogical and fanciful to contend that Judaism and Christianity ever merge as it would be to contend that heaven and earth cease to exist as separate spheres. Dispensationalism has its foundation in and is understood in the distinction between Judaism and Christianity.[2]

On this view, the Bible portrays a drama which is definitely *political* in nature; but God's political purposes are tied to the nation of Israel, as it was called to be God's special people in the Old Testament, and as it is being regathered today according to divine purposes. God's plan for Israel—which, as the dispensationalist views things, has never been canceled—is a *this-worldly* one. God has promised a land to the Jews, and he has promised to provide

[2]*Dispensationalism* (Dallas: Dallas Seminary Press, 1936), p. 41.

them with a righteous king who will rule over them in justice.

The dispensationalist admits that the Bible demonstrates a great concern for the poor and oppressed. He does not deny that Jesus is the Prince of Peace in a strongly political sense which guarantees an eventual peace among the nations. But he will insist that we cannot hope for the elimination of poverty, political oppression, and international strife apart from the peace of Israel, which will only come when Christ sits upon the Davidic throne and is acknowledged as the king of the nation Israel.

The role of the community of New Testament Christians in all of this activity is at best peripheral. God extended the offer of "spiritual" salvation to the Gentiles because the Jews rejected Jesus as Messiah during his earthly ministry. Thus, God has two plans presently in operation, which will culminate in heavenly joy for the Gentile church and earthly prosperity for the nation of Israel. New Testament Christians will not directly participate in the unfolding plan for Israel—indeed, the church will be "raptured" before God's dealings with Israel are completed. But Christians have been given the futuristic prophecies to aid them in discerning political developments as they unfold.

Several observations are in order concerning this position, which is widespread among fundamentalists, because of some typical misunderstandings of the fundamentalist posture. First, the fundamentalist-dispensationalist understanding of the special status of the Jews in God's plan for the world should make it clear that fundamentalism is not apolitical. Dispensationalism is, among other things, a *political* theology—albeit an "Israel-monistic" political theology. If dispensationalists do not take stands on many political issues which concern other Christians, it is because of their conviction that God's political purposes are intimately tied to the plight of Israel. But on this one issue, especially as it relates to the present status of the nation of Israel, few Christians have so detailed a "Christian foreign policy" as do the dispensationalists.

119

Second, the dispensationalists do not deserve to be accused, as they often are, of lacking a "social conscience." On the one issue of political importance to them, they have a very conscientious stance; indeed, they would not be afraid to cry out on behalf of Israel, even if the weight of human opinion were entirely on the other side. One suspects that a vast majority of fundamentalists would become draft-resisters if the United States declared war on Israel. (And they would no doubt offer in the process some of the most imaginative expositions of Romans 13:1-2 on record in support of their posture of civil disobedience on this matter.)

More generally, the dispensationalist position has a kind of internal consistency to it. It does not ignore those biblical passages which other Christians cite in support of a politically active position, and its political attitudes are not simply extensions of attitudes associated with the "American Way of Life." Indeed, its theology is at every point derived from the Scriptures—or at least from a way of *reading* the Scriptures. Nonetheless, there are some basic flaws in the dispensationalist approach to political matters.

For the sake of the argument, let us assume that the dispensationalist "Israel-monistic" political theology is an accurate reading of the biblical message. Are the dispensationalists, then, really justified in their political inactivism on all matters save the question of Israel? It is interesting that these same Christians believe that in the "last days" there will be developments leading to the establishment of a large "apostate church"—events which they see coming to pass in recent ecumenical developments. Here, however, dispensationalists do not sit by passively. Even though they see the emergence of false doctrine as a fulfilment of prophecy they cry out against it. Why? Because, presumably, they become restless when they encounter what they view as a perversion of the truth. Why should not this same kind of restlessness be stirred up when Christians encounter injustice, racism, and military exploitation? Does the belief that God has a special plan for Israel rule out a desire to witness against injustice and suffering wherever it appears among the peoples of the earth? Suppose one is correct in believing that we live in days when wars and suffering are inevitable. Does this belief rule out sermons in which racism and militarism are denounced?

The most basic defect in dispensationalist eschatology has to do with what might be termed a "scorecard" approach to matters of Bible prophecy, whereby the Christian seems to be little more than a passive observer checking off event after event in what he views as the prophetic scenario. Even if many of the dispensationalist assumptions are granted, it is not clear why this passive posture is adopted. Dispensationalists often view God's dealings with Israel in such a way as to imply that Christians have no business criticizing the current policies of the Israeli government. This attitude is very different from that manifested by the biblical writers. Whatever the Old Testament prophets had in mind when they articulated a vision of a glorious future for Israel, they were not afraid to criticize Israel, even to the point of denouncing policies and practices with a righteous wrath. Unlike the dispensationalists, the prophets did not allow their convictions concerning Israel's future to dull their critical sensitivities with respect to Israel's present activities.

The *fore*telling dimension of the prophetic task cannot be divorced from a desire to equip the church for its *forth*-telling ministry. The bearded, robed figure of many cartoons, with his sign proclaiming that "The end is near" comes uncomfortably close to representing a common understanding of the church's proper appropriation of biblical prophecy. This understanding is a faulty one. The church is given visions of the future not in order merely to announce that "the end" is near; nor is it provided with a secret agenda for history which it should hug to its bosom while passively awaiting its own escape from the historical process. Rather, the church is equipped with prophetic visions in order to act responsibly *in* the present, in the confidence that God has promised the ultimate triumph of justice and righteousness.

Those who have allowed an interest in "Bible prophecy" to reinforce a posture of passive futurism have failed to take two important biblical emphases into account. First, the biblical prophet articulated a vision of the future out of an intense historical involvement. Biblical foretelling arises out of what might be thought of as a dialectic of fear and hope.

The prophet is typically distressed over certain cultic practices or political policies, because of a special sensitivity to the need for purity in worship and social justice. Because he discerns idolatrous tendencies, hypocrisy, and corruption, he cries out in despair. But in the midst of his pessimism, he is comforted by the fact that God has acted decisively in the past, and he has promised to do so in the future. The prophet is strengthened by his trust that God will not fail to bring his redemptive purposes to fruition. Are there corrupt priests? Then God will send a great high priest who will bring pure offerings into the holy place. Is it difficult to find people who love justice? Well, someday justice will rush in like a mighty river. Are there perverse rulers? We need not fear: God will send a king whose very *name* is "wonderful counselor" and "prince of peace."

This "dialectical" process can be related to what J. R. R. Tolkien had in mind when he observed that "the Gospels contain a fairy-story, or a story of a larger kind which embraces all the essence of fairy-stories."[3] For Tolkien, this way of putting the matter did not constitute a denial of the historical accuracy of the Gospel accounts, for that "story is supreme; and it is true. . . . Legend and History have met and fused."[4]

Just as the coming of the Christ was, prior to its occurrence, a "fairy-story," which emerged out of the deepest

[3]J. R. R. Tolkien, "On Fairy Stories," in *Essays Presented to Charles Williams,* ed. C. S. Lewis (Grand Rapids: Eerdmans, 1966), p. 83.
    [4]*Ibid.,* p. 84.

fears and hopes of human beings, as interpreted by a prophetic sensitivity, so the as-yet-unfulfilled prophecies of the biblical message are, from our point of view, the "happy ending" projected by an exercise in imaginative wishing. None of this is meant to discount the element of *accuracy* in predictive prophecy. Rather, it is meant to illuminate the *kind* of accuracy involved. True prophecy in the biblical sense is not a mere "reading off" of the future, as if the future were already in the past or present. The prophet is not someone who curtains himself off from the world in order to gaze into a crystal ball; he is someone whose hopes are forged out of the intense agonies of historical involvement—and who is thereby made capable of discerning the shape, often in terms of images and types, of the fulfilment which the Lord of history will bring to pass.

The second emphasis which fundamentalists often ignore is the way in which predictive prophecy in the biblical context is never used to support an attitude of "fatalism." The prophet pronounces God's judgment, often in vivid detail, but in the hope that this message will elicit a response of repentance. The story of Jonah's visit to Nineveh bears this out by way of negative example; Jonah was chastened by God for his bitterness over the way in which Nineveh responded in repentance to Jonah's message of doom.

The absence of a fatalistic spirit is nowhere more obvious than in the example of Jesus. Luke tells us that Jesus, immediately after indicating to his disciples that he must die in Jerusalem, spoke of his longing to gather the people of Israel "as a hen gathers her brood under her wings; but you [Jerusalem] would not let me" (Luke 13:33-34). In the light of Jesus' conviction that his own prophesied death was inevitable, this combination of compassion for Jerusalem and the ascription of responsibility to Jerusalem is impressive. The church must follow Jesus' approach in its own dealings with human society. Even if the rejection of the prophetic message is somehow "inevitable," this is no excuse for acting as if we were the smug possessors of the secrets of history. Even in the most corrupt societies, the church's message must be a sincere pleading for justice and peace, so that we can say in good faith on behalf of our Lord: "I would have gathered you . . . but you would not let me."

## FINDING BABYLON TODAY

A second perspective which interprets current events in the light of biblical eschatological visions is represented by a certain strain of contemporary "radical Christianity." Here the crucial national entity to be assessed in the light of revealed divine purposes is not Israel but the United States. But the United States is not on this view an object of divine favor; rather, it is a prime example of the kind of national entity which will experience divine *dis*favor in the last days. In short, America is viewed as a special example of the ways of the wicked city of Babylon, whose destruction is depicted in Revelation 18.

In his recent book, *An Ethic for Christians and Other Aliens in a Strange Land*, William Stringfellow argues that Revelation's portrayal of Babylon provides us with a "parable" which reveals the condition of "death" that prevails in all "fallen" societies:

> Babylon in Revelation is a disclosure and description of an estate or condition which corresponds to the empirical reality of each and every city — of all societies — in history. The Babylon of Revelation is archetypical of all nations.[5]

For Stringfellow, however, the United States is the current successor to Nazi Germany as a special and obvious manifestation of Babylonian patterns. American life is completely given over to the way of "death"—which is a "moral reality" of corruption and destruction which can come to permeate the life of a nation. This pattern, he thinks, has

[5]*An Ethic for Christians and Other Aliens in a Strange Land* (Waco: Word, 1973), p. 48.

been characteristic of recent American foreign policy, especially in Indochina; but there are

> many other symptoms of death in America — like the apartheid stalemate in race, the prevalent waste ethic in production and marketing and consumerism, the degeneration of medical care, the emergent technological totalitarianism, the militarization of police power, the official assault against due process of law, and the proliferation of illegitimate authority.[6]

But the Babylonian pattern is not the only "moral reality" Stringfellow finds operating on the current scene. Revelation also indicates, he thinks, that we should expect to find manifestations of Jerusalem, a "holy" and "separate nation" which "lives within and outside the nations, alongside and over against the nations, coincident with but set apart from the nations."[7] While much of the institutional church is identified with the life of Babylon, Stringfellow sees hopeful signs of Jerusalem's existence in an "emerging confessional movement" represented by the "Post-Americans," the "house church" movement, some groups of prisoners, and possibly elements of the charismatic movement.

Some fundamentalist writers have also attempted to identify contemporary America with the biblical picture of Babylon, and it is interesting to compare these attempts with Stringfellow's account. In his book *Is the U. S. A. in Prophecy?*, S. Franklin Logsdon combines the references in Revelation 18 with those in Jeremiah 50-53, and produces a list of sixteen similarities between the United States and "prophetic Babylon," including a deteriorating position of world leadership, a populace made up of a "mingled people," being the youngest ("hindermost") of the nations, spiritual decadence, etc.[8]

The differences between Stringfellow's and Logsdon's

[6]*Ibid.*, p. 71.
[7]*Ibid.*, p. 52.
[8]S. Franklin Logsdon, *Is the U.S.A. in Prophecy?* (Grand Rapids: Zondervan, 1968), pp. 59f.

practical conclusions reveal one of the difficulties in the kind of attempt in which they both engage: namely, that there is a tendency to interpret the biblical descriptions of Babylon in the light of a specific ideological critique of contemporary America. Thus, Stringfellow sees America's Babylonian patterns as revealed in its militarism, racial discrimination, and unjust legal structures; whereas Logsdon worries about the United States' vulnerability to foreign "subversion," the "uprisings" of its minorities, and general patterns of "lawlessness." Happily, both accounts agree in condemning consumerism and technolatry.

Stringfellow's ideological commitment leaves him open to the criticism that he fails to note some positive tendencies in American life which, if taken into account, cast doubt on his identification of the United States with Babylon. For example, even granting the idolatrous and oppressive patterns he points to in American life, the United States has also provided in recent decades an arena for what appears to be an unprecedented and unparalleled discussion and critique of those very patterns. One wonders just who is to be identified with Babylonian America. Those members of Congress who have acted to curtail abuses of executive power, or who have exposed highly questionable "intelligence" practices? All of the black mayors of American cities? Magazines of the religious "establishment" whose pages have portrayed the hunger and suffering of the Third World?

The citation of examples of this sort is often met with the retort that nations whose corruption is carried out in very subtle ways will often allow a certain degree of self-criticism, in order to "tame" radicalism—just as long as that critique does not threaten the oppressive structures of the society. It is very difficult to assess this line of argument. It is not clear, for example, that criticism of American structures is never "allowed" to have a significant effect on those structures.

In any event, Stringfellow's identification of America as Babylon goes beyond the mere observation that the United States is very corrupt. America's Babylonian tendencies are a special manifestation of a condition shared in by all nations as *nations*: "The Fall is where the nation is. The Fall is the locus of America."[9] When Stringfellow makes the straightforward claim that "America *is* Babylon,"[10] he does not mean to imply thereby (as, for example, Logsdon does) that Revelation 18 refers to a single historical entity, namely the United States. Rather, the picture of Babylon denotes a political/cultural condition toward which all nations tend, and which the United States presently approximates in a very special way. During Hitler's day, according to Stringfellow, it would have also been correct to say, "Germany *is* Babylon." Germany of the Nazi era and contemporary America are unique in that each in its day reveals in a unique manner the dimensions of the "death" toward which all nations are progressing. Thus, Stringfellow can confidently assert: "If America *is* Babylon, and Babylon is *not* Jerusalem . . . is there any American hope? The categorical answer is *no*."[11]

Stringfellow's case can be evaluated on two levels: the empirical and the theological. Our primary concern is the latter, although we have already raised questions concerning the relationship between his analysis and the actual facts of American life. Also on the empirical level, however, we should note that critics who see only "death" in American policies and practices often ignore the important governmental "regulatory" functions whose benefits we experience on a daily basis. Thus, in the United States, official government actions set speed limits, designate one-way streets, operate traffic signal systems, provide school crossing-guards, conduct fire and safety inspections of buildings, maintain parks and rest areas, and so on. Such matters may seem trivial by comparison with issues in foreign policy and certain broad patterns of "domestic" life. But there can be no doubt that they are daily blessings that citizens experience from the hand of the state—and blessings of a

[9]Stringfellow, *op. cit.*, p. 19.
[10]*Ibid.*, p. 34.
[11]*Ibid.*, p. 155.

"life"-promoting sort. Indeed, they are matters which would have to be taken into account if the "positive" functions of the state were being assessed. And it would seem that a society's patterns in these areas would be at least relevant to the claim that the society in question is given over to the way of "death."

From a theological point of view, Stringfellow's case must be criticized, not because it draws connections between contemporary America and the biblical picture of Babylon, but rather for the rigid *manner* in which it draws those connections. Given his own view of the picture of Babylon as a "parable," it would seem that Stringfellow should say—not that America *is* Babylon—but that America, like all nations in the fallen condition, exhibits Babylonian tendencies. And to the degree that America fails to be completely Babylonian it also shows some hints—in the terms of his own distinction—of Jerusalem.

What we can say with certainty on the basis of Revelation's portrayal of Babylon's fate is that all which is truly Babylonian—in contemporary America or in any other dimension of God's creation—will ultimately be destroyed. Babylon is doomed, and Jerusalem will triumph. Of this we can be certain. But this does not make it easy for us to identify at every point the armies of each respective city. Indeed, the battle between Babylon and Jerusalem goes on in each of our hearts. The difficulties involved in identifying the opposing forces, even in this most intimate of battlegrounds, should make us sensitive to the ambiguities we must deal with in other arenas. On the basis of personal experience we should have no illusions that the self-proclaimed citizens of Jerusalem are free from Babylonian temptations. We should not be caught off-guard, therefore, when we find Jerusalem's policies being defended within the very midst of the company of the Babylonians.

How does all of this bear on Stringfellow's verdict that there is no hope for America? Here too we must evaluate his case both empirically and theologically. On empirical grounds, his verdict is not a clear one. In what sense, for example, would it have been true to say, in 1940, "There is no hope for Germany"? If this verdict had been intended as a reference to Nazi Germany, it would have been an accurate prediction. But, of course, many of the individuals and institutions which existed under Nazi rule have survived the destruction of Nazism. Is there some force analogous to Germany's Nazism in America today about which we can say, "There is no hope for *that* kind of America"? And if so, are we thereby erasing any kind of *American* hope? Assuming that Germany is less Babylonian today than it was in 1940, could the United States become less Babylonian in the next decade? Is Stringfellow intending to rule out this possibility when he issues his verdict?

One suspects that Stringfellow is making a stronger claim—such that the defeat of Nazism was *not* a sign of "hope" for Germany, just as no comparable act would introduce any kind of *American* hope. Stringfellow's case involves an attitude of hopelessness about nations as such— and perhaps even about institutions as such. We must now decide, by way of constructing our own position, whether this attitude is theologically legitimate.

## THE FUTURE OF "THE KINGS OF THE EARTH"

The dispensationalist has no hope for any nation except Israel; furthermore, he makes a radical distinction between Israel's hope and the hope of the church. Stringfellow has no hope for any nation at all; Israel, or "Jerusalem" *is* the church—but "the church" here stands for a complex of groups which function for the most part outside of the *institutional* church. What shall we say of this consensus, which we find at both ends of the theological spectrum, that Christian political hope is a hope for the destruction of the nations (with the possible exception of the Israeli nation)?

It is important to note that the portrayal of Babylon's downfall in Revelation 18 is not the Bible's final reference to the destiny of corporate powers. In the concluding vision of the Holy City's descent from the heavens, there is an allusion—a puzzling one, admittedly—to the continuing existence of *political* representatives:

> And I saw no temple in the city, for its temple is the Lord God the Almighty, and the Lamb. And the city has no need of sun or moon to shine upon it, for the glory of God is its light, and its lamp is the Lamb. By its light shall the nations walk; and the kings of the earth shall bring their glory into it, and its gates shall never be shut by day — and there shall be no night there; they shall bring into it the glory and the honor of the nations. But nothing unclean shall enter it, nor any one who practices abomination or falsehood, but only those who are written in the Lamb's book of life (Rev. 21:22-27).

The interesting reference here, for our present purposes, is to the "kings of the earth" who will bring "the glory and honor of the nations" into the New Jerusalem. What are these kings doing here? What is the point of their admission into the city?

An example of a way in which we ought *not* to interpret this reference is provided by the commentator on Revelation in *The Interpreter's One-Volume Commentary on the Bible*. He simply dismisses this as an illegitimate passage, on the following grounds:

> The continued existence of the Gentile nations after the establishment of the new era of God's rule was presupposed by the author from whom John was borrowing, and his use of this source material without adaptation creates an inconsistency. According to 19:21; 20:7-10; 20:12-15 none but faithful Christians will survive the events of the last days and the final judgment. But John often did not exert himself to remove inconsistencies.[12]

This assessment of the passage in question is inadequate for at least two reasons. First, it would seem on the face

---

[12]S. MacLean Gilmour, "The Revelation to St. John," in *The Interpreter's One-Volume Commentary on the Bible* (Nashville: Abingdon, 1971), p. 967.

of things to be extremely odd for John to be inconsistent on a matter of this sort. As one who was in exile as a result of a political policy it is highly unlikely that he would have been insensitive at the point of dealing with the future destiny of governmental authorities. And given his actual treatment of the "kings of the earth" in prior passages (which we will examine shortly), his level of consciousness while "copying" this passage would have to be lower than the dullest of scribes. Moreover, no matter how this passage relates to other elements in his narrative, we must bear in mind that in his personal salutation at the beginning of this letter to the churches, he greets his fellow believers in the name of one who is "the ruler of kings on earth" (1:5). A good case can be made for taking each element in the opening salutation as a matter to be explicated in the following material; even if that case cannot be defended on every detail, we should not be surprised that John would return here to vindicate his opening announcement that Jesus has power over earthly rulers.

Since John's critic alleges an "inconsistency" between this reference and earlier ones, however, let us briefly examine the careers of the "kings of the earth" as depicted in Revelation. The reference in the opening salutation is followed, in 2:26-27, by the promise that the faithful will be given "power over the nations" to "rule them with a rod of iron"—a promise later applied, in 12:5, to the male child born of a woman. When the sixth seal is opened (6:15-16), the kings of the earth, along with "great men and the generals and the rich and the strong," are among those who cry for the mountains and rocks to fall on them. Chapter 15:3-4, the song of Moses and the Lamb, again promises that "all nations shall come and worship" the "King of the ages."

In addition to these sporadic references, there are two major sequences involving the kings in Revelation 17—20. In 17:1-2 and 12-14, they are described as having fornicated with the harlot, and as giving their power and authority over to the beast, together with whom they will be conquered by the Lamb. In 18:9-10, after the song announcing the fall of Babylon, we see "the kings of the earth, who had committed fornication," weeping and wailing over her downfall—"stand[ing] far off."

Then in 19:17-21, the beast and the kings gather their armies for war against the armies of the horseman. The kings' armies are defeated; the beast is captured and thrown into the lake of fire, as is the false prophet—"and the rest," we are told, "were slain by the sword" of the horseman. After the thousand-year period Satan is loosed from his captivity and he comes out "to deceive the nations." Satan and the armies of the nations are again defeated; the armies are consumed by fire; and the devil is thrown into the lake of fire.

In all of this there is no direct reference to the *destruction* of the kings of the earth. They are explicitly mentioned as surviving the fall of Babylon; and although we might assume their later destruction by inference, the inference is not a binding one. At the very least, the destruction of a specific group of kings does not seem to rule out the possibility of more kings appearing later on.

The only real difficulty, then, is the puzzling presence of the kings of the earth in a situation into which "only those who are written in the Lamb's book of life" may enter. And what does it mean that they will bring "the glory and the honor of the nations" into the city? Let us consider some hypotheses.

First, we might simply infer, by conjoining the fact that only those whose names are in the book might enter in with the fact that the kings of the earth *do* enter in, that the kings have their names written in the book of life. This can be understood, furthermore, in two ways. First, it could be an indication that *all* of the kings of *all* of the nations have their names in the book. This is the view proposed by Vernard Eller:

When John deliberately puts "the kings of the earth" and "the wealth and splendor of the nations" right onto the streets of the new Jerusalem, there would seem no alternative but that he also is talking of a continued possibility of repentance and redemption, of a *"second* resurrection." And if that is a possibility for the kings of the earth — whom John, clearly, has considered as the worst of all people — then it is a possibility for anyone.[13]

Eller, then, takes this passage as evidence for his own "universalist" contention.

This is an intriguing proposal. But it is not convincing. According to Eller, the kings function here as representatives of "the worst of all people"; thus their role is, roughly, a didactic one. If they can get in, *anyone* can. But there is every reason to think that in the context their representative status is an *official* one. They enter the city, not as representatives of the dregs of humanity, but as bearers of "the glory and the honor of the nations"—a reference Eller's hypothesis does not illuminate.

A second hypothesis might be that only *some* kings will enter into the city—namely, those whose names are recorded in the book of life. It is likely that God in his mercy will have effectively brought a representative sample of political rulers to repentance during the history of civilization. Thus, we might think of the kings of Revelation 21:24 as those political leaders who are by God's grace converted sinners—who are in turn performing the official function of bringing "the glory and the honor of the nations" into the city.

This is, in fact, the interpretation given by a number of commentators who rely on the King James Version, which translates the first part of 21:24 as follows: "The nations of them which are saved shall walk in the light of it"— thereby leaving the impression that the kings involved here represent *redeemed* peoples. There is no evidence, however, for the presence of the "of them which are saved" clause in the original text. Consequently, any interpretations based on it are highly speculative.

[13]*The Most Revealing Book of the Bible* (Grand Rapids: Eerdmans, 1974), p. 200.

Our own interpretation will not assume any view of the *specific* identity of "the kings of the earth." Rather, the importance of this reference seems to reside in the significant conceptual point it makes: namely, that the coming of the kingdom of God will require an official acknowledgment on the part of human institutional authority of the sovereign rule of God.

The expectation that this kind of acknowledgment will take place is deeply rooted in the biblical message. Isaiah and Micah both use the same words to express this hope:

> It shall come to pass in the latter days
>     that the mountain of the house of the Lord
> shall be established as the highest of the mountains,
>     and shall be raised above the hills;
> and all the nations shall flow to it,
>     and many peoples shall come, and say:
> "Come, let us go up to the mountain of the Lord,
>     to the house of the God of Jacob;
> that he may teach us his ways
>     and that we may walk in his paths."
> For out of Zion shall go forth the law,
>     and the word of the Lord from Jerusalem.
> He shall judge between the nations,
>     and shall decide for many peoples;
> and they shall beat their swords into plowshares,
>     and their spears into pruning hooks;
> nation shall not lift up sword against nation,
>     neither shall they learn war any more.
>                     (Isa. 2:2-4; Mic. 4:1-3)

The Apostle Paul seems to have a similar eschatological requirement in mind when, in Philippians 2:10-11, he says that Jesus has been given "the name which is above every name," at which "every knee should bow, in heaven and on earth and under the earth, and every tongue confess that Jesus Christ is Lord, to the glory of God the Father"—a theme repeated in Philippians 3:21, where Christ's resurrection power is described as a force which "enables him even to subject all things to himself."

However we interpret the reference to the thousand-year period in Revelation 20, we must credit the millennial tradition—in both its "pre-" and "a-millennial" forms—for recognizing this important conceptual requirement. Millennialists have rightly insisted that it is not enough for Christ to rule in the hearts of the saints; his rule must be manifested in the transformation of political processes as we now know them. George Eldon Ladd provides the correct rationale for this insistence: "Christ is now reigning as Lord and King, but his reign is veiled, unseen and unrecognized by the world. . . . His reign must become public in power and glory and his Lordship universally recognized."[14]

By admitting the kings of the earth into the city, then, John seems to be acknowledging this conceptual requirement and giving expression to the fulfillment of a deeply rooted biblical hope.

## "THE GLORY AND THE HONOR OF THE NATIONS"

It is important to note, however, that the conceptual requirement we have been discussing has to do with more than a mere political transaction. The kings of the earth are political representatives; but they are more than that. When they bring "the glory and the honor of the nations" into the new Jerusalem they are acting as representatives of the diverse cultures which have developed in the course of history.

Two elements of the picture must be emphasized here. First, the kings of the earth represent only one of several kinds of authority whose presence is acknowledged in John's description. In Chapter 21:12 he tells us that the twelve gates of the city have the names of the tribes of Israel written on them; and in 21:14 the twelve foundations of the city are said to bear the names of the twelve apostles. Thus, with the entrance of the kings of the nations, the new

[14]George Eldon Ladd, A Theology of the New Testament (Grand Rapids: Eerdmans, 1974), p. 630.

**135**

Jerusalem absorbs the life and the authority of some major institutions—tribe, church, nation—which have developed in history.

Second, as we have already noted above, the kings themselves represent more than political power. The Bible's references to "nations" are intended to single out *peoples,* with all of the cultural richness and diversity associated with that term. Institutional life, even *political* institutional life, is surely included here—but not to the exclusion of such phenomena as art, literature, religious practices, and other cultural expressions. We would not be entirely misled if we thought here of the Wise Men from the East, who followed astrological guidelines in order to bring their gifts to the infant Jesus.

What is the *point* of this transaction—the bringing of "the glory and the honor of the nations" into the city? Here also there are two factors which ought to be emphasized. First, they bring their cultural splendor into a *city*. It has been observed by many writers that the biblical drama begins with a garden and ends with a city. Herein lies the Bible's recognition of the fact of cultural development. When the end-time comes there will be an acknowledgment that the historical process has occurred, with all that this means in terms of cultural and institutional life. This is an important consideration to keep in mind, especially because of the subtle—and not-so-subtle—varieties of anti-institutionalism which regularly tempt the Christian community. In some sense, historically-developed institutions will be "received" into the kingdom of God. They will not be merely forgotten or destroyed.

Second, we cannot answer the question concerning the point of the transaction with the kings without bringing in the additional element referred to in Revelation 22:2-3: "On either side of the river, the tree of life with its twelve kinds of fruit, yielding its fruit for each month; and the leaves of the tree were for the healing of the nations. There shall no more be anything accursed."

Isaac Watts was correct when he wrote that the Savior

136

"comes to make his blessings flow/Far as the curse is found." And Revelation indicates that the curse not only influences the life of the nations, but that the *removal* of the curse will extend to national entities. But what will be the *character* of the event or process described as "the *healing* of the nations?*"

Any answer to this question must be speculative. This much seems clear, however: it is at least possible that political institutions as we now know them—along with various other structures and activities associated with the culture-building life of a people—will not be destroyed in the last day, but will be purified and transformed into fitting dimensions of the kingdom of God. If this is the proper way to view matters, it is not enough to say, as we observe the institutions and practices of our political/cultural life, "Created, but *fallen.*" We must also say, "Fallen, but *created.*"

The proper question, then, is not—as Stringfellow puts it—How can we live humanly during the fall? There is a more complicated question that we must ask: How can we live humanly in a created-but-fallen world which will some day be restored in accordance with God's good purposes? As it applies to political life this is not an easy question to answer. Because we look for a city which is yet to come, we will not be able to place our ultimate trust in the systems of the present age. But because the tree may sprout leaves for the healing of the kinds of nations of which we are presently citizens, we cannot completely dissociate ourselves from that which God has promised to heal.

## THE TRANSFORMATION OF POLITICS

The thesis we have been developing in this chapter, and indeed throughout this book, was well formulated in its general intent by H. Richard Niebuhr:

[Human] culture is all corrupted order rather than order for corruption. . . . It is perverted good, not evil; or it is evil as perversion, and not as badness of being. The problem of culture is therefore the problem of its conversion, not of its replacement by a new creation; though the conversion is so radical that it amounts to a kind of new birth.[15]

Niebuhr's final clause—"the conversion is so radical that it amounts to a kind of new birth"—symbolizes some of the ambiguities that remain in the formulation of our own position in this book. What, in the final analysis, is the difference between a "new birth" and a "radical conversion?" How does the "transformationalist" approach we have adopted differ in practice from that which looks for a thoroughly new creation which will come into being after the anticipated destruction of the present order?

Many of the differences here have to be spelled out on the level of attitude and mood as they related to present political involvement. If our hope is to be articulated in terms of "the healing of the nations," as we are insisting, we must proceed in the confidence that participation in the structures and institutions of the present age is not a mere "holding action" but a legitimate means of *preparation* for life in the kingdom which is yet to come in its fulness.

We would not deny the tensions and ambiguities involved in the perspective we have been developing; indeed, we would insist that these tensions and ambiguities, properly understood, reflect similar ones in God's own attitude toward the present condition of his creation. To put it in another way, our attitudes toward present-day institutions and cultural patterns must be neither more optimistic than God's nor *less* optimistic.

Human cultural activity, of which political decision-making is an important dimension, was an implicit presence in the creation which God originally pronounced to be "good" (Gen. 1:31). And it will be a visible element in the new order which will someday hear him announce: "It is done! I am the Alpha and the Omega, the beginning and the end" (Rev. 21:6). Our present involvement in his cre-

[15]H. Richard Niebuhr, *Christ and Culture* (New York: Harper, 1951), p. 194.

ation—even in the structures of human culture—must be carried out with the proclamations of Genesis and Revelation echoing in our spiritual ears.

But we must not operate with a triumphalism that is deaf to yet another divine cry: the "It is finished" of the cross. Here the victory-cry of God—itself poised between his announcements at the original creation and the final restoration of all things—absorbs the hurts and agonies of the fallenness of his creation, not in order to wallow in sin, nor merely to condemn the rebellious world, but that the world might be saved through his own suffering.

Christian political involvement must take place before the cross, and it must be a means of sharing in the agonies of the cross. But it must also be carried on in the *hope* that God will allow our present activities to count as preparatory signs of his coming kingdom. This hope would be impossible to attain if it were not for the continuity of the healing promised for the nations with a healing process which has already begun—whereby those who put their trust in Jesus Christ as Lord and King become "like a tree planted by the streams of water, that yields its fruit in its season, and its leaf also does not wither" (Ps. 1:3). It is because of this experience that we look for the fulfilment of the promise offered to the Apostle on Patmos, a promise extended to both individuals and "the nations": "Blessed are those who wash their robes, that they may have the right to the tree of life and that they may enter the city by the gates" (Rev. 22:14).

# INDEX OF PRINCIPAL SUBJECTS

Anabaptist thought, 98-99
athletics, 64-65
business practices, 65
Calvinism, 99, 103-105, 107
capitalism, 45
ceremony, 60-63
Christian politicians, 66
Church,
    as community, 60-61, 63-64
    as institution, 56, 59, 61, 63-64
    "invisible," 63
    and kingdom, 63-64
    as organism, 59
    "visible," 63
coercion, 32, 35, 85, 104, 109-110
covenant partnership, 27-28
Cross of Christ,
    as "payment," 114
    and political hope, 139
    see also Powers
"discipline," church, 57, 110
dispensationalism, 118-124
"dominion," 26-28, 33, 105, 108
eschatology,
    and "Babylon," 124-129, 132
    and institutions, 129, 136, 138
    and Israel, 118-121
    scope of, 117

fatalism, 123-124
God,
    as despot, 39-41, 45
    knowledge of, 9-10
    as Triune, 25, 29, 53
government, nature of, 32-36,
    102-107
hierarchy, 32, 35-36
idolatry, 44, 89-90
"imitation of Christ," 112-116
individualism, 22, 30, 55
justice, 78-79
"kingly" activity, 67-68, 70, 80, 85
Marxism, 9, 51-52
millennialism, 135
moral decision-making, 107-109
New Jerusalem, 130-131, 135-137
normative egoism, 42
oppression, 49-50, 70-74, 80, 110
organic metaphors, 31, 55-56
patriarchy, 32, 34-35
politics, scope of, 16
poor, 74-77
possessions, 76-77
Powers,
    and angels, 87-88
    and Cross, 91-92, 111-112, 114-
        115

and institutions, 88
ontology of, 94-97
preaching, 57
proclamation, 67-70
prophetic task, 122-124
psychological egoism, 41-44
sacraments, 57
servanthood, 67-70
sexuality, 16-17, 46, 78-79
sin,
   as ethical rebellion, 37
   institutionalized, 46-47, 49-50

as self-deception, 37-39
and selfishness, 41-45
socialism, 45
sociality, 22-32, 55
"state of nature," 29-30
subordination, 100-101, 113-114
theocracy, 104-106
theology,
   divisions of, 13-15
   "political," 10-11, 14-15
United States, 124-129
universalism, 133

# INDEX OF SCRIPTURE REFERENCES

**Old Testament**

Genesis 22, 30, 32, 139
1   28
1:6   94
1:26-27   23
1:28   26
1:31   138
2:18   23
2:20   23
2:23, 25   23
3:5   39
3:16-19   45
5   27, 28
5:1   25
7:11   94
9:6-7   53
11:4   49
17:7   53

Exodus
14:21   94
23:20-21   82

Deuteronomy
15:11-15   74n.

Joshua
24:13   74

1 Samuel
8:7   105
12:14   105

Psalms   94
1:3   139
8   27, 28
8:4-8   26
72:1-4   106
89:6-8   87
93   93
93:3-4   94
139:23-24   50

Isaiah
2:2-4   134

Jeremiah
29:7   106

Daniel
4:27   106
12:1   87

Joel   13

Amos   13
1   106

5:11   75
5:11-12   75

Micah
4:1-3   134

**New Testament**

Matthew
9:11   72
25:31-46   75

Mark
4:39   94

Luke
1:52   75
13:33-34   123
15:1-2   72
18:18-30   77
19:5   76

John
1:14   41
14:15-17   82
21:12   135
21:14   135

Romans
1:18, 20-21    38
1:23    44
8:38-39    86, 90, 95
12-13    75n.
12:4-5    31
13    90
13:1    90
13:1-2    120

1 Corinthians
2:8    90

Galatians
4:3    90
4:9    90

Ephesians
6:12    86, 90

Colossians    90
1:16    86
2:13-15    114

2:15    91
2:19    91n.

1 Timothy
2:1-2    106
2:11    32
5:16    75

Philippians
2:10-11    134
2:27-28    41
3:21    134

James
2    75

1 John
3:2    56

Revelation    139
2:26-27    131
4:6-8    94
5:9-10    114

6:15-16    131
12:5    131
15:3-4    131
17-20    131
17:1-2    131
17:12-14    131
18    127, 129
18:3    75
18:9-10    132
19:17-21    132
19:21    130
20    135
20:7-10    130
20:12-15    130
21:4-5    40
21:6    138
21:22-27    130
21:24    133
22:2-3    136
22:3-4    32
22:3-5    33
22:14    139